New Frontiers in Space

The Reference Shelf
Volume 91 • Number 5
H.W. Wilson
A Division of EBSCO Information Services, Inc.

Published by
GREY HOUSE PUBLISHING
Amenia, New York
2019

The Reference Shelf

The books in this series contain reprints of articles, excerpts from books, addresses on current issues, and studies of social trends in the United States and other countries. There are six separately bound numbers in each volume, all of which are usually published in the same calendar year. Numbers one through five are each devoted to a single subject, providing background information and discussion from various points of view and concluding with an index and comprehensive bibliography that lists books, pamphlets, and articles on the subject. The final number of each volume is a collection of recent speeches. Books in the series may be purchased individually or on subscription.

Publisher's Cataloging-In-Publication Data
(Prepared by The Donohue Group, Inc.)

Names: Grey House Publishing, Inc., compiler.
Title: New frontiers in space / [compiled by Grey House Publishing].
Other Titles: Reference shelf ; v. 91, no. 5.
Description: Amenia, New York : Grey House Publishing, 2019. | Includes bibliographical
    references and index.
Identifiers: ISBN 9781642652222 (v. 91, no. 5) | ISBN 9781642652178 (volume set)
Subjects: LCSH: Astronautics--United States. | Outer space--Exploration--United States. |
    Space warfare--United States. | Space tourism--United States. | United States. National
    Aeronautics and Space Administration.
Classification: LCC TL789.8.U5 N49 2019 | DDC 629.40973--dc23

Printed in Canada

Contents

3

Legacy of the Space Race

4

NASA and the International Space Station

5

Space in Popular Culture

Preface

The Next Frontier

Space is a limitless void. The stars and their planets occupy only a minute fraction of this endless expanse and, as of 2019, humanity knows of only one planet with the rare collection of elements needed to support life as we know it. Since before recorded history, humans have dreamed of exploring the cosmos, perhaps finding extraterrestrial life or establishing human colonies in the distant reaches of the galaxy. Presently, such aspirations are still strictly within the realm of science fiction and yet, the innate desire to explore the unknown continues to drive the question of whether humanity will ever venture beyond the confines of Earth.

The journey into space began after World War II, when the propulsion systems used to create the world's first ballistic missiles for warfare were repurposed for the scientific effort to explore the universe beyond Earth's atmosphere. Initially, this effort was fueled by nationalistic interests. The former Soviet Union and the United States competed to develop space travel technology in the Space Race of the 1960s, with both nations hoping for a military advantage. Due to fluctuations in political climate and priorities, interest in space science waxed and waned, and the United States has advanced little since the early 1970s. In the 2010s, however, public outlook on space has begun to change again, and an increasing number of scientists and politicians are urging for a new surge in space exploration. This new era of space science is heavily driven by private companies, the commercialization of space, military development. Together, these factors are contributing to the perception that America might be entering a new Space Age.

Military Might and Corporate Profit

Two significant forces in the recent push for space exploration have aligned in the 2010s. In 2018, President Trump called for the formation of a sixth branch of the U.S. armed forces focused on defending U.S. assets in space. Trump is not the first president to urge for the militarization of space, and recent developments in technology has meant that the potential for hostile encounters in space—such as attacks on commercial or governmental satellites—has become a reality. Trump's plan called for the "Space Force," a multi-billion-dollar program that would have created the first new branch of the military since the establishment of the Air Force in 1947. However, Trump was forced to settle for the establishment of a new and largely symbolic branch within the Air Force which is currently in charge of managing American military defense of space.[1]

Trump's push for space militarization led to a number of other nations questioning their own military presence in space. France and China both announced plans to engage in space defense development.[2] As of 2019, military space technology is still in its infancy. The United States and many other nations operate a number of satellites performing both military and commercial functions. The most immediate goal of military space development would be to protect these assets, though most of the nations involved are also seeking to revive an idea first developed in the 1970s and 80s, that space-based technology could be used to prevent or deter nuclear attacks from terrestrial sources.

The second major development sparking renewed interest in space is space tourism, an emerging field in which a number of private companies are developing new technology—including craft capable of leaving and reentering Earth's atmosphere—or are partnering with other organizations to utilize existing technology. The ultimate goal is enabling private individuals to travel to space. As of 2019, there are few vehicles, anywhere in the world, that have been tested and proven to travel back and forth into space. A small number of companies, including Space X and Virgin Galactic, are in the final phases of testing technology that will be used to create a space tourism industry but nothing is ready for general consumption. The most basic space tourism packages cost about $50 million, restricting the market to the extremely wealthy. Even within that market, additional challenges limit the appeal of space travel. Those interested in becoming one of the first to tour space recreationally must not only pay millions, also endure more than six months of difficult training to make a journey that is extremely physically demanding and dangerous.

Once in space, the only viable location to visit is the International Space Station (ISS), a facility constructed between 1998 and 2011 through a cooperative effort between five different space agencies. The National Aeronautics and Space Administration (NASA) estimated that the ISS would be viable only through 2015, but the facility has remained in working order, surpassing the expectations of experts. NASA recently expanded the life expectancy of the station through 2024, in part because of space tourism. Beginning in the early 2000s, a company called Space Adventures began taking the first civilian tourists to space, where they were allowed to visit the ISS. Though the Trump administration has announced plans to divest American interest in the station, the potential for the ISS to host space tourists is helping to maintain interest in keeping the station functioning and active. Most recently, in June of 2019, NASA released a proposal to sell packages in which tourists will fly aboard a NASA vehicle and then stay aboard the ISS; the basic entry price is $59 million, which includes approximately $35,000 per night aboard the International Space Station.[3]

The militarization and commercialization of space occupy a unique position in human culture, as both fields have cross-ideological appeal. While conservatives are more likely to embrace the need for militarization due to a pro-military industrial worldview, moderates and some liberals might also see value in protecting the increasing number of valuable space resources used for science and commercial purposes. Likewise, the commercialization of space appeals primarily to those who favor private market development and corporatization, but there are aspects of commercialization with more generalized appeal. For instance, researchers in China (and to a lesser degree in the United States) are interested in utilizing advanced satellite technology to gather energy from the sun in space. While practical development in this field is distant, research suggests that harvesting energy from space might be more efficient than any terrestrial method, therefore helping to solve the climate change challenge.[4]

The Past and Future

2019 marked the fiftieth anniversary of the first moon landing, and NASA and its partners, as well as many of the world's independent space agencies, hosted events and programs to commemorate this momentous achievement. New articles about the Apollo Program helped introduce a new generation to this tumultuous and innovative period and to the goals of the ongoing effort to study and explore space. With this flurry of coverage, readers worldwide were invited to consider how the interplay between economics, political campaigning, and military insecurity have played a role in the development of space science, and how much these elements should guide the development of space technology in the future.

NASA seized on public interest in the organization's past successes with the Apollo Program to discuss the organization's future plans. Among a wide variety of scientific projects, NASA is beginning operations for a series of new space vehicles, and has plans to again send astronauts to the moon as early as 2024. Even before the Apollo Program met its untimely end in 1972, the goal of exploring Mars was a leading priority for NASA. The idea that the Martian landscape may harbor life intrigued humans centuries before the first close-up images became available and before NASA succeeded into obtaining the first surface data from the planet via automated rovers. The planet has long occupied a central place in human mythology and remains a primary target for space science. NASA has plans to land another rover on Mars in 2021[5], which will be equipped with new tools to search for evidence of microbial life. The search for extraterrestrial life remains a dominant strain of interest in space science, and NASA has plans to conduct detailed studies of Jupiter's moon Europa and Saturn's moon Enceladus, both of which contain ice and potentially liquid salt water, and may therefore harbor simple life beneath their frozen surfaces. The search for extraterrestrial life has drawn contributions from many spheres of science and remains among the most marketable to the public.[6]

While NASA and private organizations are concentrating on testing new passenger ships and automated tools for studying space, the renewed interest in space has reignited discussions of the enduring idea that humanity should visit and potentially colonize Mars. In the 1950s, as the seeds of NASA were first being sowed, researchers and engineers were influenced by science fiction. Experts in both the United States and the Soviet Union imagined that, possibly even within their lifetime, humans could be living in high-tech bases on the moon or on Mars. The effort to enable human astronauts to explore Mars is still a leading goal for NASA and many space scientists. However, with the vast expansion of reliable information on

Mars gathered since the 1950s, scientists now know just how difficult engaging in a manned mission to the planet would be, to say nothing of the possibility of settling there.

Writing in *Gizmodo*, George Dvorsky summarized the challenges of colonizing the "Red Planet," noting that Mars is a cold, dead planet with a toxic atmosphere, deadly temperature swings, and insufficient gravity to support the internal workings of the human body. Many experts feel that, unless major changes occur in the development of space technology, a realistic human colony on Mars would be unlikely to occur within the next millennium. Dvorsky reasons that one of the reasons interest in colonizing Mars may be growing is that humanity worldwide is increasingly aware that the growing population is incompatible with Earth's resources and are therefore drawn to models that might alleviate this situation.[7] Astrophysicist Martin Rees, in his book *On the Future: Prospects for Humanity*, dissuaded Americans from this way of thinking about humanity's future, arguing:

"It's a dangerous delusion to think that space offers an escape from Earth's problems. We've got to solve these problems here. Coping with climate change may seem daunting, but it's a doddle compared to terra-farming Mars. No place in our solar system offers an environment even as clement as the Antarctic or the top of Everest. There's no 'Planet B' for ordinary risk-averse people."

Space tourism might also contribute to climate change, as researchers have begun to note that a massive increase in space flight will likely provide a highly negative contribution to global warming, on a par with commercial air travel. As the new wave of space development is spearheaded by corporations, who have entered the market searching for profit, will these companies engage in responsible development and invest in technology to ensure that the commercialization of space doesn't come at a further cost to Earth's ecosystems? Before committing to the void of space, Americans must attempt to solve some of the world's dire terrestrial problems, or there is a risk that the frontier of space becomes little more than another, less hospitable battleground.

Works Used

Dvorsky, George. "Humans Will Never Colonize Mars." *Gizmodo*. Jul 30, 2019. Retrieved from https://gizmodo.com/humans-will-never-colonize-mars-1836316222.

Erwin, Sandra. "Defense Intelligence Report: China in Steady Pursuit of Space Capabilities to Outmatch U.S." *Space News*. Jan 16, 2019. Retrieved from https://spacenews.com/defense-intelligence-report-china-on-steady-pursuit-of-space-capabilities-to-outmatch-u-s/.

Insinna, Valerie. "Trump Officially Organizes the Space Force under the Air Force . . . For Now." *Defense News*. Feb 19, 2019. Retrieved from https://www.defense-news.com/space/2019/02/19/trump-signs-off-on-organizing-the-space-force-under-the-air-forcefor-now/.

"MARS 2020 Mission." *NASA*. 2019. Retrieved from https://mars.nasa.gov/mars2020/.

"NASA's Plans to Explore Europa and Other 'Ocean Worlds'." *Phys Org*. Mar 6, 2017. Retrieved from https://phys.org/news/2017-03-nasa-explore-europa-ocean-worlds.html.

Sowers, George. "Commercializing Space: Before a Commercial LEO Market Can Flourish, the ISS Must Be Retired." *Space News*. Mar 19, 2019. Retrieved from https://spacenews.com/op-ed-commercializing-space-before-a-commercial-leo-market-can-flourish-the-iss-must-be-retired/.

Whitcomb, Isobel. "NASA Wants to Let Space Tourists Onto the Space Station—for $59 Million." *Live Science*. Jun 7, 2019. Retrieved from https://www.livescience.com/65670-nasa-iss-space-tourism.html.

Notes

1. Insinna, "Trump Officially Organizes the Space Force under the Air Force . . . For Now."
2. Erwin, "Defense Intelligence Report: China in Steady Pursuit of Space Capabilities to Outmatch U.S."
3. Whitcomb, "NASA Wants to Let Space Tourists Onto the Space Station—for $59 Million."
4. Sowers, "Commercializing Space: Before a Commercial LEO Market Can Flourish, the ISS Must Be Retired."
5. "MARS 2020 Mission," *NASA*.
6. "NASA's Plans to Explore Europa and Other 'Ocean Worlds'." *Phys Org*.
7. Dvorsky, "Humans Will Never Colonize Mars."

1
Visions of Space

By Official SpaceX Photos, via Wikimedia.

Elon Musk's SpaceX, pictured above, is the first private company to send a spacecraft to the ISS, and one of many companies developing space technology for tourism and other commercial ventures. This photo was taken during Iridium-4 launch operations.

Space For Sale

The exploration of space has resulted in a wealth of scientific data that has transformed many aspects of life. Developments in space technology have led to the invention of new consumer products and, as technology evolves, a number of entrepreneurs are looking at ways to increase the monetization of space. As of 2019, this includes "space tourism," the now famous effort to open space travel to consumers. There are other opportunities for profit as well, including the possibility of harvesting natural resources from space to potentially alleviate resource shortages on Earth.

Touring Space

The 1960s proved that human spaceflight was possible, raising the prospect of recreational space travel. In the early 1970s, Rockwell International, the company contracted by the U.S. government to work on the design for NASA's space vehicles, began looking into the possibility of creating a passenger cabin for space flight. They imagined this housed in a shuttle's cargo bay and holding 74 passengers for a 3-day journey orbiting the earth.

In the 1980s, NASA began experimenting with allowing non-governmental astronauts to accompany crews on Space Shuttle missions through its "Space Flight Participant" program, which was intended to gradually open up the experience of space to the civilian world. Charles Walker, an employee of aerospace manufacturing firm McDonnell Douglas, traveled aboard a space shuttle flight in 1984 as the first non-governmental astronaut to fly on an American spaceflight. The program hit a major setback in 1985, when teacher Christa McAuliffe was killed along with the crew when the space shuttle *Challenger* tragically exploded on take-off. The *Challenger* disaster was a setback not only for the idea of civilian space flight, but for the U.S. Space Program as a whole. Space shuttle missions were put on hold for two full years and the Space Flight Participant program was completely abandoned.

The 1990s saw the beginning of development in space tourism in earnest. The first company to enter the market was SpaceDev, which was founded in California in 1997 and later purchased by the Sierra Nevada Corporation. The first company to successfully offer civilian space tourism was Space Adventures, which was founded in 1998 in Virginia. Space Adventures utilizes Russian space technology and has secured permission to send individuals to the International Space Station (ISS) aboard Russian *Soyuz* spacecraft. The company sent their first client—U.S. entrepreneur Dennis Tito—into space aboard a *Soyuz* craft in 2001, making Tito the world's first space tourist. Tito reportedly paid $20 million for the opportunity and underwent more than six months of training at the Yuri Gagarin Cosmonaut Training Center at Russia's Star City. Following Tito's successful trip, Space Adventures sent a small number of other clients into space, including Tito for a second trip, making him the first two-time space tourist.

The most recent client scheduled for a flight with Space Adventures was wealthy English singer Sarah Brightman, who began training for her flight (which carried a reported price of $52 million) in 2015. However, it was soon announced that Brightman had either postponed or cancelled her trip. Writing in *Time Magazine* in May 2015, Jeffrey Kluger speculated that though space tourism had become a reality, the process—both for preparation and during an actual voyage into space—was so difficult that participants, even barring the extreme cost, were likely to remain limited. As Kluger explained:

> On both the way up and the way down, the crew can pull more than 4 g's (4x the gravity of earth), and that's only if everything goes well. In 2008, cosmonaut Yuri Malenchenko and astronaut Peggy Whitson were coming home aboard a Soyuz when the rear part of the spacecraft—the service module—failed to separate as it was supposed to. That sent them on what's called a ballistic reentry of 30 degrees, causing them to pull a torturous 8 g's. The near-fatal plunge took 23 minutes to unfold. Even the best Soyuz reentry has been described by astronaut Scott Kelly, who is aboard the ISS for a marathon one-year stay and had been looking forward to Brightman's visit, 'like going over Niagara Falls in a barrel—that's on fire'.[1]

As Kluger notes, the space flight technology available in the 2010s ensures that space tourism remains both difficult and dangerous. To participate in Space Adventures programs, clients are required to participate in a minimum of six months of difficult training and additional training (at an additional cost) for optional activities. Despite these difficulties, the success of Space Adventures paved the way for a host of other companies. In the late 1990s, XCOR Aerospace and Bigelow Aerospace both entered the market. In 2002, controversial billionaire Elon Musk ventured into the field with the foundation of his SpaceX company, which planned to focus on innovative new space vehicles in addition to space tourism. This was followed by the entry of billionaire Amazon founder Jeff Bezos' Blue Origin company in 2004, and then billionaire Richard Branson's Virgin Galactic Rocket Laboratory in 2006.

As of 2019, most of the initial companies that entered the space tourism industry have failed to achieve any measurable success. In 2006, industry pioneer Space Adventures announced that the company would begin offering "space walks" for visitors to the ISS at an additional cost of $15 million; as of yet no tourist space walks have been conducted. Progress in space tourism stalled considerably in October 2014 when Branson's Virgin Galactic suffered the crash of its *VSS Enterprise* test vehicle, resulting in the death of one pilot and severe injuries to another. Despite this tragedy, Virgin Galactic emerged as one of the most viable space tourism companies of the 2010s. The company finally reached space in 2018 with a crew of two trained astronauts, becoming the first company to successfully launch a privately developed manned space vehicle. Though the flight only lasted 16 minutes, and the crew consisted of veteran test pilots C.J. Sturckow and Mark Stucky, the victory was a major step forward in terms of proving the viability of the company's plans.[2] In 2019, Virgin Galactic became the first space tourism company to go public, drawing $800 million in investment from Branson through his Social Capital Hedosophia Holdings Corp, which the company announced would provide funding until it could begin turning a profit.[3]

Criticisms of space tourism programs are centered primarily on the prohibitively high cost, which thus far means that even the most basic space tourism options are available only to the extremely wealthy. Further, current technology poses limitations and makes civilian space flight difficult and dangerous, thus further limiting the recreational value and broader public interest in the industry. These concerns may be overshadowed by an emerging scientific concern: that space tourism and the repeated use of rockets to break Earth's atmosphere might contribute markedly to climate change. A 2010 study published in *Geophysical Research Letters* raised this concern after data suggested that the atmospheric impact of commercial space flight would be comparable to commercial air travel, which is one of the most significant contributors to global warming overall. Particles emitted by rockets used in space flight might remain in the stratosphere of the Earth for as long as a decade, eventually raining down and contributing to pollution. Space tourism companies have yet to create plans to address the potential environmental impact of their activities, but this is a major concern that must be addressed as the industry moves forward or space tourism companies might find themselves at odds with the scientific community.[4]

Other Commercial Opportunities

Space tourism is the most popular topic in the field of space commercialization, but there are other ways to take advantage of extraterrestrial resources. One of the most promising is the potential to harvest solar energy directly from space, thereby removing the atmospheric obstacles that complicate the collection of solar energy from the Earth's surface. This emerging field, known as Space-Based Solar Power (SBSP), is not currently a reality, but a significant number of scientists have suggested that such a method might prove a viable way to eliminate reliance on fossil fuels.[5]

The idea of collecting solar energy from space is older than many might realize. Visionary science fiction author Isaac Asimov is often credited with inspiring interest in this process with his 1941 short story "Reason," which featured a space station designed to harvest energy from the sun and transmit it to planets using microwaves. Solar powered satellites became a reality in the 1970s thanks to improvements in systems for collecting and storing solar energy. Between 1976 and 1980, NASA spent $50 million on a study of SBSP and another major feasibility study was done in the 1990s, which concluded in 2000. At that time, the scientists involved in the program concluded that achieving SBSP using a large solar power satellite (SPS) would require significant advancements in current technology. However, the team laid out a potential road map for how this might be achieved over a period of decades.[6]

Works Used

Fernholz, Tim. "Virgin Galactic Makes It to Space." *Quartz*. Dec 13, 2018. Retrieved from https://qz.com/1494884/richard-bransons-virgin-galactic-reaches-space/.

Howell, Joe T. and John C. Mankins. "Preliminary Results from NASA's Space Solar Power Exploratory Research and Technology Program." *NTRS*. Jan 01, 2000. Retrieved from https://ntrs.nasa.gov/search.jsp?R=20000044328.

Kluger, Jeffrey. "What Sarah Brightman's 'Postponed' Mission Says About Space Tourism." *Time*. May 13, 2015. Retrieved from https://time.com/3857685/sarah-brightman-space-tourism-mission/.

Mann, Adam. "Space Tourism to Accelerate Climate Change." *Nature*. Oct 22, 2010. Retrieved from https://www.nature.com/news/2010/101022/full/news.2010.558.html.

Nankivell, Kirk. "Why the Future of Solar Power Is from Space." *Singularity Hub*. Dec 31, 2018. Retrieved from https://singularityhub.com/2018/12/31/why-the-future-of-solar-power-is-from-space/.

Porter, Jon. "Virgin Galactic to Become the First Space Tourism Company to Go Public." *The Verge*. Jul 9, 2019. Retrieved from https://www.theverge.com/2019/7/9/20687323/virgin-galactic-publicly-traded-richard-branson-space-tourism-profitability.

Notes

1. Kluger, "What Sarah Brightman's 'Postponed' Mission Says About Space Tourism."
2. Fernholz, "Virgin Galactic Makes It to Space."
3. Porter, "Virgin Galactic to Become the First Space Tourism Company to Go Public."
4. Mann, "Space Tourism to Accelerate Climate Change."
5. Nankivell, "Why the Future of Solar Power Is from Space."
6. Howell and Mankins, "Preliminary Results from NASA's Space Solar Power Exploratory Research and Technology Program."

Super Fast Travel Using Outer Space Could Be $20 Billion Market, Disrupting Airlines, UBS Predicts

By Michael Sheetz
CNBC, March 18, 2019

UBS believes there will be very lucrative ramifications from the space flight efforts currently led by Virgin Galactic, SpaceX and Blue Origin.

A lengthy UBS report published on Sunday found that, in a decade, high speed travel via outer space will represent an annual market of at least $20 billion and compete with long-distance airline flights. Space tourism will be a $3 billion market by 2030, UBS estimates.

"While space tourism is still at a nascent phase, we think that as technology becomes proven, and the cost falls due to technology and competition, space tourism will become more mainstream," UBS analysts Jarrod Castle and Myles Walton wrote in the note. "Space tourism could be the stepping stone for the development of long-haul travel on earth serviced by space."

UBS expects the broader space industry, which is worth about $400 billion today, will double to $805 billion by 2030 when accounting for these innovations. While these sub-sectors would be a small part of that, Castle and Walton said "the outlook for the space economy, space tourism and long-haul travel using space has become much more bullish."

Private space companies "are investing aggressively across the space opportunity," UBS said, and the firm believes access to space "is the enabler to broader opportunities for investment."

Revolutionizing Long Distance Travel

Long haul airplane flights that are more than 10 hours in duration would "be cannibalized" by point-to-point flights on rockets, UBS said. The firm pointed to SpaceX's plans to use the massive Starship rocket it is building to fly as many as 100 people around the world in minutes. SpaceX said that Starship would be able to fly from New York to Shanghai in 39 minutes, rather than the 15 hours it takes currently by airplane.

UBS estimates that there are more than 150 million passengers a year that fly routes longer than 10 hours. Last year, those routes saw 527,000 routes on airplane that had an average of 309 seats, UBS said.

"If we assume that 5 percent of these flights in the future are serviced by space at $2,500 per trip, the revenue opportunity as of today would be more than $20 billion per year as of today," UBS said

"Although some might view the potential to use space to service the long-haul travel market as science fiction, we think ... there is a large market," UBS said.

UBS noted that "it is unlikely that a rocket will carry over 300 people anytime soon," so the Starship's capacity of 100 will be the maximum for the foreseeable future. However, UBS believes there may be an "increased frequency of space travel during the day to enable the same volume of passengers," the firm said.

> **More than 10 percent of people in a recent UBS survey said they would choose a spacecraft over an aircraft for long distance travel.**

"Given the length of long-haul commercial travel, and the rules around crewing and take-off and landing time slot restrictions at airports, we think a re-usable rocket (especially if not land-based) would have materially better utilisation rates than a commercial plane," UBS said.

As a result, UBS believes the $20 billion estimate "could prove conservative," the firm said. More than 10 percent of people in a recent UBS survey said they would choose a spacecraft over an aircraft for long distance travel.

"While the timing of such a long haul service is uncertain, we think our base-case assumptions are conservative," UBS said.

Space Tourism's Market Potential

The billions of dollars pouring into private space companies represents "a high level" of capital formation, UBS said. Even though space tourism "is still nascent," UBS said they believe the sub-sector "will become mainstream as the technology becomes proven and cost falls."

To date, space tourism has largely been limited to the few flights organized by U.S.-based Space Adventures. Over the past two decades, the company has flown seven tourists using Russian Soyuz rockets. At a reported cost of more than $20 million per person, the private clients typically spent over a week on board the International Space Station.

But now "there are a number of commercial space ventures to open up suborbital travel," UBS noted. Virgin Galactic and Blue Origin are leading those efforts, both getting steadily closer to launching paying tourists.

"This area seems to be the market that has the greatest potential to gain traction quickly," UBS said.

Virgin Galactic is deep into the development program of its spacecraft. Last month, the space venture owned by Sir Richard Branson sent test passenger Beth

Moses on Virgin Galactic's spaceflight—a first for a private U.S. company. Virgin Galactic's spacecraft holds up to six passengers along with the two pilots. As the company has more than 600 would-be astronauts signed on to launch, Moses' work is key to preparing Virgin Galactic for commercial operations. Tickets for Virgin Galactic's flights are priced at $250,000 each.

UBS believes Virgin Galactic's business model, as both a tourism company and manufacturer of spaceships, mimics the growth of businesses in the early days of aviation.

"In this way history could repeat itself as United Airlines today can trace back its roots to the Boeing Aircraft & Transport Company," UBS said.

Blue Origin, the company founded by Amazon CEO Jeff Bezos, is also nearing its first spaceflights with human passengers. Blue Origin is developing the New Shepard rocket system for the company's space tourism business.

As both Virgin Galactic and Blue Origin utilize reusable spacecraft systems, UBS believes the companies will be able to make space tourism "a more common occurrence" as reliability increases and prices decline.

"We estimate space tourism will be a $3 [billion plus per year] opportunity growing at double digit-rates," UBS said. "This would be similar to what happened in commercial aviation, especially after the rise of low-cost airlines."

SpaceX could also see significant cash flow from space tourism, UBS believes, through two different ventures. Elon Musk's company just completed a historic test flight of its Crew Dragon capsule, which will be able to send as many as four astronauts to the space station. UBS estimates that NASA will pay SpaceX about $58 million on average per astronaut, compared to the $81 million per astronaut for flights on Russian Soyuz rockets.

The second SpaceX opportunity is for early flights of Starship to send tourists on missions beyond the Earth's immediate orbit. In September, Musk announced Japanese billionaire Yusaku Maezawa signed with SpaceX to fly around the moon on Starship. Maezawa expects to fly in 2023, with six to eight guests joining him for the flight.

Print Citations

CMS: Sheetz, Michael. "Super Fast Travel Using Space Could Be $20 Billion Market, Disrupting Airlines, UBS Predicts." In *The Reference Shelf: New Frontiers in Space,* edited by Micah L. Issitt, 7-9. Amenia, NY: Grey House Publishing, 2019.

MLA: Sheetz, Michael. "Super Fast Travel Using Space Could Be $20 Billion Market, Disrupting Airlines, UBS Predicts." *The Reference Shelf: New Frontiers in Space,* edited by Micah L. Issitt, Grey Housing Publishing, 2019, pp. 7-9.

APA: Sheetz, M. (2019). Super fast travel using space could be $20 billion market, disrupting airlines, UBS predicts. In Micah L. Issitt (Ed.), *The reference shelf: New frontiers in space* (pp. 7-9). Amenia, NY: Grey Housing Publishing.

Moon 2069: Lunar Tourism and Deep Space Launches a Century on from Apollo?

By Monica Grady

The Conversation, July 31, 2019

We've just celebrated the 50th anniversary of the first moon landing, glorying in the achievements of three astronauts and the team of engineers and scientists behind them. From that perspective, we can look back and see what we have learned from the mission. But what if we take a giant leap forward in time and look back at the legacy of Apollo from 2069—a century after the historic event?

It was thanks to the rocks collected by the Apollo astronauts that scientists could work out the age of the moon, its evolutionary history and how the Earth and other planets evolved. Continued study of the samples, complemented with new information from orbiting spacecraft, also showed that the moon was not the dry and desiccated body we had thought.

Rather, the moon has abundant water reservoirs, stored as ice below its surface and in shadowed craters at the poles. There's also water locked within specific minerals and absorbed into the lunar soil from impacts of tiny meteorites.

This finding led to a resurgence in the idea of the moon as a starting point for exploration of the further reaches of the solar system. That's because water can also be used as a fuel. If you separate the hydrogen and the oxygen that make up water, you can then let the two gases react with—this is essentially what goes on in a rocket engine. The oxygen can also be used to provide breathable air for astronauts, opening up new opportunities for habitation and long-distance space travel alike.

But how do you extract these gases from water ice? The moon's permanently shadowed regions are close to areas that are sunlit for more than 80% of the time. If the sunlight could be harvested using solar panels, sufficient energy could be generated for electrolysis—chemical decomposition splitting the extracted water into pure hydrogen and oxygen by passing an electric current through a liquid or solution.

Current Plans

Today, discussions about lunar exploration have moved away from establishment of a permanent lunar base as a preliminary for extended exploration. Instead, there has been a significant advance in planning the construction of the Deep Space

Gateway—a space station in orbit around the moon. This is an international project between a number of different space agencies.

Commercial companies are also playing an important role in this project, which is much more than an extension of the International Space Station. The spacecraft will be a hub of scientific and engineering activity. It will be serviced by the Orion module and will act as a test bed for astronauts preparing for longer duration missions, such as to Mars. Missions could also eventually be launched from there, saving money on fuel as the rockets won't have to make it through the Earth's enormous gravity.

All this activity would require a spaceport, not just for transfers between the Earth and the moon, but also for spacecraft using the moon as a Launchpad for exploring further afield.

The experiments scientists could do there—such as monitoring the external environment of the moon, including radiation levels—would certainly help prepare us to send missions to Mars and beyond. And testing the physiology of astronauts in a low gravity environment would not only be of use for planning future space missions, but may also lead to the development of medical interventions to alleviate the effects of ageing.

Different space agencies have separate visions for how lunar exploration could progress, with varying levels of detail published. NASA's programme of lunar exploration is based on using the gateway to facilitate a regular series of visits to the moon by astronauts. The European Space Agency has a similar set of objectives and is working closely with Russia's Roscosmos to drill at the lunar south pole and with Japan's JAXA to return samples from the moon.

Resources available on the moon's surface include metals from the lunar soil (especially titanium) and solar energy to provide power. This could eventually enable infrastructure to be built, allowing humans to create an actual lunar base soon—even though plans are now focussing on getting the gateway done first. One exciting possibility that is actively being explored is the idea of a lunar base built from modules that are 3D printed on the lunar surface using fuel extracted from the lunar soil as an energy source and building material.

Most Likely Scenario

Between 1969 and 1972, 12 men landed on the moon, spending, in total, just over three days exploring the lunar surface. They planted the flag of a single nation, collected rocks and undertook a few simple experiments. Between 2019 and 2069, what might we actually hope to see? A permanent, international lunar base on the moon's surface, surrounded by flags of all the nations involved, would certainly be possible.

There would have to be refreshed space law to make this possible though, including a specific Lunar Treaty reinforcing the idea that only peaceful use of the moon is permitted, that international cooperation is paramount and commercial exploitation of resources forbidden. Currently, the legal framework is contradictory and confusing.

There would most likely be a changing roster of (male and female) astronauts of all nationalities in continuous occupation of this base. They would be not be "astronauts" per se though. They would be scientists undertaking experiments and collecting data from instruments based on the moon (including the far side) as well as engineers designing, building and maintaining infrastructure for further exploration, plus ancillary support staff. A regular shuttle service would operate between the lunar surface and the Deep Space Gateway and also between Earth and the Deep Space Gateway, for personnel and resources.

It is likely that the tourist trade will be burgeoning, necessitating a transport infrastructure on the lunar surface, plus a hotel, with its attendant caterers, cleaners, tour guides and so forth.

All this activity would require a spaceport, not just for transfers between the Earth and the moon, but also for spacecraft using the moon as a launchpad for exploring further afield. Indeed, by 2069, we could be seeing the start of regular journeys to Mars.

This will be too late for me: by 2069, my travelling days will be over—I will be 111 years old. But maybe if the medical benefits from occupation of the moon are transferred into terrestrial health services, I might still be sufficiently alert to receive messages from my grandson and his family as they holiday on the moon.

Print Citations

CMS: Grady, Monica. "Moon 2069: Lunar Tourism and Deep Space Launches a Century on from Apollo?" In *The Reference Shelf: New Frontiers in Space,* edited by Micah L. Issitt, 10-12. Amenia, NY: Grey House Publishing, 2019.

MLA: Grady, Monica. "Moon 2069: Lunar Tourism and Deep Space Launches a Century on from Apollo?" *The Reference Shelf: New Frontiers in Space,* edited by Micah L. Issitt, Grey Housing Publishing, 2019, pp. 10-12.

APA: Grady, M. (2019). Moon 2069: Lunar tourism and deep space launches a century on from Apollo? In Micah L. Issitt (Ed.), *The reference shelf: New frontiers in space* (pp. 10-12). Amenia, NY: Grey Housing Publishing.

Soon, Hundreds of Tourists Will Go to Space: What Should We Call Them?

By Eric Berger
Ars Technica, March 4, 2019

Perhaps within a matter of a months, a handful of customers will board a spacecraft and fly above Earth's atmosphere to float for a few minutes, where they will presumably gawk at our planet's graceful curvature. Shortly after this, dozens, and soon hundreds, will follow. Space enthusiasts have made such promises about space tourism for nearly a decade, but in 2019 it's *finally* coming true.

In the last three months, Virgin Galactic has completed two crewed test flights above 80km. And with its flight-tested New Shepard launch system, Blue Origin remains on track to blast its own people into space later this year. Both spacecraft can carry up to six passengers. Neither company has begun commercial operations, but these flights appear imminent. Later this year, suborbital space tourism should finally transition from long-promised to something you can do if you're rich enough. Next year, we will likely see dozens of commercial flights.

These Welcome Successes Have Raised a Question, However: Just What Do We Call These People?

Until now, it has been fairly easy to call men and women who have gone to space astronauts (or cosmonauts in Russia, and taikonauts in China). About 560 humans have gone to space, nearly all of them into orbit, and a lucky two dozen have gone beyond. Twelve have walked on the Moon.

In 2004, the private SpaceShipOne venture clouded the picture a little bit by making a private suborbital flight. The pilots, Mike Melvill and Brian Binnie, had not trained as government astronauts, so the US Federal Aviation Administration created a new designation for them—commercial astronauts. Since then, the five crew members of Virgin Galactic's VSS Unity flights in December and February have also earned that designation. But the FAA will only recognize "crew," not passengers.

For now, there remains no official word on what to call non-crew members. Are they astronauts, too? Space passengers? Astro-nots? In the hopes of finding a consensus, we put that precise question to the companies, some bonafide NASA astronauts, and some experts in the aerospace community.

Defining Space

This is *not* a story about the definition of space. For a long time, the generally accepted boundary of space was 100km, the so-called the Kármán line. This artificial barrier is recognized by the Fédération Aéronautique Internationale, the international record-keeping organization for aerospace. But this view is not unanimous, as the US Air Force delineated 80km as "space" for its participants in the X-15 rocket plane program.

For Virgin Galactic, this is a salient issue, because its tourist flights are likely to reach a peak altitude above 80km, but below 100km. In all of its promotional materials, the company has referred to anything above 80km as space. Harvard University astrophysicist Jonathan McDowell, has argued that orbiting objects can survive multiple perigees at altitudes around 80 to 90km and that this altitude range is consistent with the highest physical boundary of the atmosphere, the mesopause. An altitude of 80km, McDowell says, is consistent with the lower boundary of space.

Virgin's primary competitor in suborbital space tourism, Blue Origin, sees its guarantee of a flight above 100km as a valuable marketing point. The company will fly that high, founder Jeff Bezos said, because it does not want there to be any "asterisks" next to its customers' names when it comes to astronaut designation.

"One of the issues that Virgin Galactic will have to address, eventually, is that they are not flying above the Kármán line," Bezos said at a Wings Club luncheon in February. "The vehicle isn't quite capable. So for most of the world, the edge of space is defined as 100 kilometers. In the US, it's different. But I think that one of the things that they will have to figure out is how to get above the Kármán line."

The purpose of this story is not to litigate the boundary of space, however. Rather, it is to discuss what to call people who buy tickets on suborbital vehicles. They're not trained astronauts. (Many of NASA's best and brightest recruits train for five years, or more, before launching). They're not crew. Mostly, they simply had the disposable funds to buy a ticket, a free weekend, and the fortitude to strap themselves to a rocket.

The Marketers

Not surprisingly, Virgin Galactic and Blue Origin both believe people who buy their tickets—$250,000 for Virgin, and an as-yet undisclosed amount for Blue—should justifiably call themselves astronauts. We asked each company for its rationale why. Here was Virgin Galactic's response:

> As you know, at Virgin Galactic our customers pre-flight are Future Astronauts and post-flight they will be Astronauts.

> Why? Because throughout history, any human who has flown above a certain altitude, regardless of whether it's orbital or sub-orbital, [has] been called astronauts—or cosmonauts or taikonauts. Nonetheless, as a proud US and European brand, we're delighted to stick with astronaut and follow the tradition set.

And here is what we received from Blue Origin:

> Those who fly with Blue Origin will be called astronauts. They'll be trained for space-flight and will travel above the Kármán line, the internationally recognized boundary of space, joining the rank of other astronauts who have done the same.

There are few surprises in these responses, so now let us turn to some other stakeholders in the aerospace community.

NASA Astronaut View

Perhaps the best people to ask about this question are some of the astronauts who have gone to space and returned as evangelists for sharing the wonders of space with those back on Earth.

Nicole Stott flew two missions to space, spending more than three months on the International Space Station in 2009, then serving as a mission specialist on space shuttle Discovery's final flight in February 2011. During her stint on the station, Stott became the first person to paint what she saw out the window while in space. Later, after retiring from NASA, she became a founder of the Space for Art Foundation.

"I think it's simple: if they get to 'space,' they're an astronaut," she told *Ars*. "We're at a time where the opportunity for traveling to space is opening up to more people. Whether you are traveling to space as a professional who lives and works there or as someone just visiting, it seems the simplest approach is the best."

Over time, this may need to evolve, she said. When there are many people living, working, and visiting space, there may need to be some distinction between the space professional and the visitor classification. But for now, "astronaut" works for everyone. This seems significant, coming from Stott, who was selected as an astronaut in 2000 and flew into space after nine years of training.

Several alternatives to "astronaut" have been modified for people who will fly on vehicles under development to reach space: they might be called "space tourists," "space flyers," or "space travelers."

"I don't mean to discount the significant difference in preparation and requirements associated with the professional versus visitor, because I don't believe that can be argued," she said. "I just don't think there's any value debating a name."

Stott is encouraged by the prospect of more people visiting space, because she thinks more people being exposed to the "overview effect" will help more of humanity realize that we all live on a single blue-green planet, that we're all in it together, and the only border that matters is the thin blue line of atmosphere that blankets humanity.

Another former NASA astronaut and year-2000 classmate of Stott's, Terry Virts, expressed similar views about the importance of more people sharing the experience of spaceflight. After two missions, including a three-month tour as commander of the space station, Virts authored *A View From Above* to share photos of Earth that he took from the station.

Virts is also is fine with calling everyone astronauts. Someone who learns to fly a glider is a pilot, just as a 747 captain or F-16 pilot is also a "pilot," even though there is an enormous difference between them, Virts noted. So the same reasoning should apply to astronauts.

"If someone straps on a rocket and launches themselves into space and then survives re-entry and landing on Earth, I think they have earned the title of astronaut," he said. "There is of course an enormous gap between a short ballistic flight and a flight into orbit—as there is between a short-duration mission versus a long-duration one and a flight to the Moon or even Mars—but that doesn't take away the fact that they flew into space."

What Is the Alternative?

During the early days of air travel, both commercial flight crews and their passengers were called "aviators," but over time that use went away. A similar phenomenon may occur with space travel, as more and more people fly high.

This may come when suborbital flight is used more like an airline. Aside from tourism, one relatively near-term aspiration of Virgin Galactic (and SpaceX, with its much larger Starship vehicle) is point-to-point travel that would carry people one-quarter or half-way around the world in less than an hour. That may well be the stage at which any designation of "astronaut" for suborbital flight gives way to "passenger," but we're not there yet.

Several alternatives to astronaut have been mooted for people who will fly on Virgin's VSS Unity, Blue's New Shepard capsule, and other vehicles under development to reach space. Generically, they might be called "space tourists," "space fliers," or "space travelers."

There are bureaucratic options, too. In the past, NASA has called self-funded fliers such as multimillionaire Dennis Tito, who bought access to the International Space Station via a Russian Soyuz spacecraft, "spaceflight participants."

"That is bland and bureaucratic, and I don't think it should be used outside of NASA memoranda," said McDowell, the Harvard University astrophysicist. He prefers the term astronauts but might allow for a distinction between professional astronauts and some other designation such as private astronauts.

Among those we spoke with, perhaps the most acceptable alternative to astronaut was "space tourist." This is accurate, reflecting that someone has gone to space and paid their own way, and it is useful for distinguishing a passenger from crew. However, it is not particularly sexy. What would you rather be—an astronaut like Neil Armstrong, or an Instagram influencer-turned space tourist?

We're Going with "Astronauts"

The aerospace community first confronted this naming question after Tito's privately-funded flight the space station in 2001, said Robert Pearlman, editor of the

CollectSpace website. Pearlman was director of marketing for Space Adventures, which organized the trip for Tito and six other private individuals who followed on Soyuz missions to the station, for up to two weeks, through 2009. Despite NASA's clinical title of "spaceflight participant," given their extended training and crew activities, these ISS visitors generally came to be regarded as astronauts.

But the current iteration of space tourism is clearly different. Trips to space won't cost $40 million but will be closer to a quarter of a million dollars. They won't last for two weeks, but 10 minutes. And it won't be a handful of people but at least hundreds. In the eyes of some, these new weekend dabblers in spaceflight won't quite have earned the "astronaut" label.

What seems clear is that the flight providers, Virgin and Blue, intend to call their ticket buyers "astronauts." It seems likely that the participants, themselves, will want to be called astronauts as well. Suborbital flights have a lot to offer those who take them—a kick in the seat from lighting a rocket engine, weightlessness, and of course the view from the heavens above. But perhaps, above all, there is the cachet of becoming an "astronaut" in name, something that fewer than 600 humans can claim throughout the history of this world.

Part of the attraction of these commercial suborbital flights, at least to some and at first, will be the opportunity to return home as an "astronaut," Pearlman said. "And maybe that is what they should be called until the activity graduates from being a feat or stunt to one of day-to-day life."

The media is likely to default to what the companies and fliers call themselves, unless someone official—NASA, the US Air Force, or the Fédération Aéronautique Internationale—issues a kind of firm directive saying otherwise. This seems unlikely.

So we're ready to welcome the hundreds and perhaps thousands of new "astronauts" coming home from space in the next few years. Truthfully, they're supporting commercial spaceflight efforts by paying a premium up front. Ultimately, by doing so, we hope they're helping to democratize access to space for the *rest of us* in years to come.

Print Citations

CMS: Berger, Eric. "Soon, Hundreds of Tourists Will Go to Space: What Should We Call Them?" In *The Reference Shelf: New Frontiers in Space,* edited by Micah L. Issitt, 13-17. Amenia, NY: Grey House Publishing, 2019.

MLA: Berger, Eric. "Soon, Hundreds of Tourists Will Go to Space: What Should We Call Them?" *The Reference Shelf: New Frontiers in Space,* edited by Micah L. Issitt, Grey Housing Publishing, 2019, pp. 13-17.

APA: Berger, E. (2019). Soon, hundreds of tourists will go to space: What should we call them? In Micah L. Issitt (Ed.), *The reference shelf: New frontiers in space* (pp. 13-17). Amenia, NY: Grey Housing Publishing.

Space Tourism Could Have Big Impact on Climate

By David Chiga

New Scientist, October 26, 2010

Space tourism could have major consequences for Earth's climate. New computer simulations suggest soot emitted by the rockets could raise temperatures at the poles, significantly reducing seasonal ice cover there, but uncertainty remains about the assumptions used in the study.

In the next few years, space tourism companies hope to start routinely flying passengers on suborbital space flights. Now, Martin Ross of the Aerospace Corporation in Los Angeles, California, and colleagues have performed the first detailed simulations of the flights' effects on Earth's climate.

They assumed a flight rate of 1000 suborbital trips per year, the number put forward in business plans for space tourism in 2020, and estimated the emissions from a rubber-burning engine like that planned for Virgin Galactic's SpaceShipTwo.

The researchers found that the effect of soot, which is incompletely burned fuel, would dwarf that of the carbon dioxide emissions from the launches. Soot readily absorbs sunlight, warming the atmosphere where it is abundant.

Above the Weather

The 1000 annual launches would belch out about 600 tonnes of soot, or black carbon—less than today's output from airplanes and other sources. But plane soot occurs at low enough altitudes for rain to wash it out of the atmosphere in just days or weeks. Rockets expel the stuff at altitudes three times as high—in the stratosphere more than 40 kilometres above sea level. There, well above the weather, it can remain for up to 10 years.

To study the effects of black carbon emissions, Ross's team used a 3D simulation of Earth's climate. They assumed that all the black carbon is emitted over Spaceport America, a space tourism hub being constructed in New Mexico, US.

The researchers found that the black carbon caused temperatures to rise at the north and south poles. The increase was about 0.2 °C for most of the year, but peaked at around 1 °C during each hemisphere's winter. The extra warmth caused sea ice at each pole to melt, especially in Antarctica, where the area covered by ice shrank by as much as 18 per cent in the summer.

Ozone Connection

Team member Michael Mills of the National Center for Atmospheric Research in Boulder, Colorado, says the team is still trying to understand exactly why the black carbon emissions would cause warming at the poles.

But the soot should warm air in the stratosphere, and this could strengthen currents there that carry air from the equator to the poles.

That would reduce the amount of ozone over the tropics and increase it over the poles—an effect seen in the simulation. That increase in polar ozone might be responsible for the polar warming, Mills says, pointing out that the converse has been observed on Earth—polar cooling is associated with decreases in ozone over Antarctica. The connection is probably due to the way ozone interacts with radiation, he adds, though researchers are still trying to understand the exact mechanism.

"It's not a pretty picture for the Arctic or Antarctic," says Charles Zender of the University of California, Irvine, who says the new study was "very carefully done."

Educated Guess

Mills admits there is still uncertainty about the study's findings. He notes in particular that the team lacked data on how much black carbon would be emitted per flight by space tourism vehicles. The team assumed that Virgin Galactic's rubber-burning engine would emit 60 grams of black carbon per kilogram of fuel burned.

However, the team did not have access to measurements of black carbon emissions from Virgin Galactic's engines, or those of other space tourism companies, which plan to burn other types of fuel, such as kerosene.

> **The researchers found that the black carbon caused temperatures to rise at the north and south poles.**

Lacking emission measurements from rubber-burning rockets, the researchers extrapolated from data on kerosene-burning rockets. These suggested soot emissions of 20 to 40 grams of black carbon per kilogram. Rubber is expected to burn less cleanly, but it is not clear by how much—the 60 grams is an educated guess.

Newer and Cleaner

Jeff Greason, CEO of XCOR Aerospace, based in Mojave, California, which is developing a suborbital tourism vehicle called the Lynx, questions the accuracy of the soot emission estimates used in the study.

The soot data they used for kerosene rockets appear outdated and "at least an order of magnitude higher" than other measurements suggest, Greason says.

Modern kerosene-burning engines like those used in the Lynx are cleaner, he says. "The soot generation is so low that it is difficult to measure it," he told *New Scientist*. "So much of the data out there seems to come from older rockets with more soot generation."

Print Citations

CMS: Chiga, David. "Space Tourism Could Have Big Impact on Climate." In *The Reference Shelf: New Frontiers in Space,* edited by Micah L. Issitt, 18-20. Amenia, NY: Grey House Publishing, 2019.

MLA: Chiga, David. "Space Tourism Could Have Big Impact on Climate." *The Reference Shelf: New Frontiers in Space,* edited by Micah L. Issitt, Grey Housing Publishing, 2019, pp. 18-20.

APA: Chiga, D. (2019). Space tourism could have big impact on climate. In Micah L. Issitt (Ed.), *The reference shelf: New frontiers in space* (pp. 18-20). Amenia, NY: Grey Housing Publishing.

Space Tourism's Rubbery Rockets May Spur Climate Change

By Dave Mosher
Wired, October 29, 2010

Suborbital spaceflights that rely on rubber-based rocket fuel could shrink icecaps, alter the ozone layer and affect global temperatures, according to a new study.

Yet the study authors' assumptions about the number of rocket launches per year and the chemistry of rocket exhaust have raised questions about their conclusions among space-tourism companies and climatologists not involved in the study.

Atmospheric scientists who performed the research probed the effects of belching ultrafine soot high into the stratosphere, where—unlike the troposphere below it—there isn't rain and wind to quickly filter soot out of the air. Rubber-based rocket fuel burned with nitrous oxide is the preferred propellant of the burgeoning space-tourism industry, and chemists suspect such hybrid engines emit sooty black carbon. Closer to Earth, the stuff has been shown to soak up extra radiation from the sun and contribute to climate change.

"This study was a natural extension of the climate-research community gaining a greater and greater appreciation of black carbon in terms of global radiative forcing," said Martin Ross, an atmospheric scientist at the Aerospace Corporation in El Segundo, California, and leader of the research funded in part by his employer. "Soot is a very large issue in the troposphere," Ross said, but its behavior isn't well-understood at higher altitudes.

To model the effects of space tourist launches on the Earth's atmosphere, Ross and his colleagues used the open-source Whole Atmosphere Community Climate Model Version 3, or WACCM3, one of the most-advanced computer models available to study impacts to global climate.

They ran two supercomputer-powered simulations for two weeks, one as a control and another modeling the impact of 1,000 suborbital flights per year for the next four decades. That many flights, according to the study, would annually deposit more than 1.3 million pounds of soot into the stratosphere.

"We looked at the stated business plans from corporations that are planning to build vehicles for space tourism," Ross said. "If you go to their websites, they'll say things like, 'we plan to launch once per day.' We found 1,000 per year is well within stated objectives of the industry."

On average, according to the simulation, the soot pushed polar ocean temperatures up by 1.8 Fahrenheit degrees, melted 5 to 15 percent of sea ice and depleted 1 percent of tropical ozone (while boosting polar ozone by 6 percent).

"We're not making any particular prediction about any system, just taking reasonable guesses at what soot from a hybrid rocket engine looks like and what the launch industry will do in the future," Ross said. "When we put that into a gold-standard model, the effect on the Earth is surprisingly large. In short, we think black-particle carbon from rockets is something that deserves attention."

Their assumptions may not be perfect, said Gerald North, an atmospheric scientist at Texas A&M University who was not involved in the study, but the measured effect is significant enough to warrant further investigation.

While they make assumptions about some unknowns, such as the behavior of soot at high altitudes, North said, "they're careful in expressing this is not the last word" and are "inviting others to take a look."

Ross and Michael Mills, an atmospheric chemist at the National Center for Atmospheric Research in Colorado and a co-author of the study, said that's precisely what the research team sees as the next step. In particular, getting a handle on what's in the emissions of different types of rocket plumes.

"There are few direct high-altitude measurements of rocket plumes. We really need to get aircraft in those and get measurements of soot and other particles," Mills said. "Until then, the sophistication of our models is limited."

> **The impact of 1,000 suborbital flights per year for the next four decades... would annually deposit more than 1.3 million pounds of soot into the stratosphere.**

To do just that, Ross said The Aerospace Corporation is planning a workshop to bring together under one tent all the stakeholders in science, rocket engineering, space-tourism companies and the government agencies.

"We need to get these players together and exchanging ideas, then ask the policy people to figure out what to do, if anything, with the information," Ross said.

"I think we and others in the industry welcome the opportunity to talk about all of these issues," said George Whitesides, CEO of Virgin Galactic, a space-tourism company that's planning to use hybrid rocket engines. Whitesides wasn't without reservations about the study and its conclusions, however.

"Frankly, I have to admit I wished they talked to us before putting out a paper, but that's OK. Climate issues are deeply important to Virgin, and we take them very seriously," Whitesides said.

Part of the reason the company chose the hybrid rocket design for its SpaceShipTwo was "because of its significantly lower environmental impact than other designs." Whitesides also said 1,000 space tourist launches per year is "guesswork," because the industry is privatized and young.

"I think as we look at this more, we'll find the impact will be far smaller than that set out in the paper," he said. "In any case, I welcome the conversation."

Whether or not peaceable collaborations ensue, both Ross and Mills expressed that carbon soot is something the nascent space tourism industry can't ignore.

"This shows that a new kind and level of emission being deposited directly into the stratosphere could have a significant effect," Mills said. "Companies need to proceed with developing their systems with full knowledge of consequences on the planet."

Print Citations

CMS: Mosher, Dave. "Space Tourism's Rubbery Rockets May Spur Climate Change." In *The Reference Shelf: New Frontiers in Space,* edited by Micah L. Issitt, 21-23. Amenia, NY: Grey House Publishing, 2019.

MLA: Mosher, Dave. "Space Tourism's Rubbery Rockets May Spur Climate Change." *The Reference Shelf: New Frontiers in Space,* edited by Micah L. Issitt, Grey Housing Publishing, 2019, pp. 21-23.

APA: Mosher, D. (2019). Space tourism's rubbery rockets may spur climate change. In Micah L. Issitt (Ed.), *The reference shelf: New frontiers in space* (pp. 21-23). Amenia, NY: Grey Housing Publishing.

China Plans a Solar Power Play in Space That NASA Abandoned Decades Ago

By Eric Rosenbaum and Donovan Russ
CNBC, March 17, 2019

John Mankins has spent his professional life working on novel ideas that could transform the way humans use technology in space, solar power among them. But Mankins' interplanetary musings went beyond the way solar is already used to power satellites and the International Space Station. During a 25-year career at NASA and CalTech's Jet Propulsion Laboratory, he devised multiple concepts to extend the use of solar in space, among them a solar-powered interplanetary transport vehicle and a space-based power system.

It's that second idea, in particular, that had Mankins' attention while holding top research positions at NASA during the 1990s and 2000s, including overseeing the $800 million Exploration Systems Research and Technology group. Mankins—who now runs his own private aerospace firm, Artemis Innovation Management Solutions—had the task of figuring out whether there was a way to deliver electricity to the planet by beaming it from space. It's an idea that could fundamentally reshape the idea of the utility business—and give control over it, on a global scale, to whichever world power gets there first.

"If you can dramatically lower the cost of space solar, you can take over most of the energy market of the world," said Mark Hopkins, a member of the National Space Society board of directors and former Rand Corp. executive.

Mankins got close to seeing the idea make it into reality, with support from the Bush White House and Congress in the 2000s, and positive reviews from the National Academy of Sciences and a national security unit within the Department of Defense. But the program never took flight, for a variety of reasons. So when the news recently broke that the idea—abandoned decades ago by NASA—was coming back to life with a big push from government, it was cause for excitement. But it isn't NASA finally backing the idea. It's the Chinese government.

The Space Race Heats Up

China's ambitions in space rival that of the United States. Its two main objectives were originally human spaceflight (accomplished in 2003) and a permanent Chinese space station, which is coming closer to reality—it announced in early March that a manned space station similar to ISS is now on schedule for 2022, earlier than expected.

As the two geopolitical foes increasingly turn their attention to a technological and military race beyond the earth's atmosphere, space-based solar power projects are an overlooked, often criticized idea. But with China recently announcing that within the next decade it expects to finish the high voltage power transmission and wireless energy tests that would be needed for a space-based solar power system, the concept is likely to get renewed attention.

> **This is not posturing; this is a real plan from serious organizations with revered scientists in China. They have a perfectly good technical plan, and they can do it by 2030.**
> **John Mankins**
> PRESIDENT OF SPACE SYSTEMS AND TECHNOLOGY FIRM ARTEMIS INNOVATION MANAGEMENT SOLUTIONS

All of the plans in the space race have potential implications for a new military build-out in space of increasing relevance to the world's powers. The Trump administration formalized plans in February for a branch of U.S. military known as the Space Force. The solar power station plans being contemplated by China include the launch of small- to medium-sized solar power projects in the stratosphere to generate electricity between 2021 and 2025, followed by a space-based solar power station that can generate at least a megawatt of electricity in 2030, and a commercial-scale solar power plant in space by 2050.

"The dramatically stated interest on the part of the Chinese will do a lot to engender interest," Mankins said. "Around a decade ago the Chinese started working seriously on this, and about five years ago they started coming to international meetings. Before that, they were in the dark. Now they are coming out of the shadows and talking much more openly about this." He added, "There is absolutely progress from the Chinese at this point. This is not posturing; this is a real plan from serious organizations with revered scientists in China. They have a perfectly good technical plan, and they can do it by 2030," Mankins said, describing a small-scale solar power project producing megawatts of electricity, but not a commercial-scale project able to produce gigawatts needed to compete with utilities.

A space-based solar power station would capture the sun's energy that never makes it to the planet and use laser beams to send the energy back to Earth to meet energy demand needs. China said in a recent announcement about the project that a big advantage of space-based solar power is its ability to offer energy supply on a constant basis and with greater intensity than terrestrial solar farms.

One of the issues with renewable-energy projects like solar and wind power plants are their intermittency—that refers to the fact that the sun isn't shining and the wind is not blowing 24-hours a day, limiting the periods of time during which these projects can be a source of power generation.

Space-based solar would not only offer a solution to intermittency, but also delivery. Today, utility power generation is regional, if not local, but electricity generated in space and near the equator could be beamed almost anywhere across the globe, except for the poles. "You could beam electricity from Canada to the Tierra del Fuego at the southern tip of South America from a satellite at equator," Mankins said. Roughly one billion people live in the Americas.

Hopkins said the current Chinese view is, "We want to be major dominant power in space solar power by 2050. This has the potential to really turn the geopolitics in our favor if we are a leader, so let's look at it seriously." Meanwhile, the U.S. says, "Are you kidding? Let's worry about something else."

New Life for a 'Losing Proposition'

The idea of collecting solar power in space was popularized by science fiction author Isaac Asimov in 1941 in a short story that envisioned space stations that could transport energy from the sun to other planets with microwave beams. In 1968, Asimov's vision was brought closer to reality when an American aerospace engineer named Peter Glaser wrote the first formal proposal for a solar-based system in space. After experimenting in the 1970s with transporting solar power, Glaser was able to land a contract with NASA to fund research. However, the project suffered with changes in federal administrations and it was not until 1999 that NASA's solar power exploratory research and technology program jumped back in to study the issue.

In the end "NASA didn't want to do it," Mankins said. But a lot has changed, especially relating to the cost equation and rapid advances in technologies like robotics.

A NASA spokeswoman said it is not currently studying space-based solar power for use on Earth. It is exploring several advanced power and energy technologies to enable long-duration human exploration of the Moon and Mars, such as its Kilopower project, a small, lightweight nuclear fission system that could power future outposts on the Moon to support astronauts, rovers and surface operations. Next year, this project is expected to transition from ground-based testing to an in-space demonstration mission.

Historically, the cost of rocket launches and the weight that would be required for a project of this scale, made the idea of space-based solar unfeasible. There are scientists who still hold that view today.

"The energy, mass and cost budgets involved show that this is a losing proposition, not just now but perhaps for centuries to come," said Olivier L de Weck, a professor of Aeronautics, Astronautics and Engineering Systems at the Massachusetts Institute of Technology. "The energy we need to put in to launch the mass required for the SBSP [spaced-based solar power] station is so enormous that we may never recoup it."

Mankins said this view is becoming quickly outdated due to a dramatic lowering of rocket launch costs through efforts funded by billionaires including Tesla founder Elon Musk's SpaceX and Amazon founder Jeff Bezos's Blue Origin. Meanwhile, developments in robotics and modular-manufacturing—being able to produce many small modular pieces to make a whole rather than one huge piece of equipment—could lead to cost-effective ways to construct these projects in orbit without having to build a multi-billion-dollar factory in space. He referenced a major review conducted by the federal government in 1981 that when looked at in today's dollars would have cost up to $1 trillion to deliver the first kilowatt/hour of solar from space. "The whole program was killed in the U.S.," he said.

Now the studies conducted on feasibility are decades old and simply no longer relevant to the discussion, Mankins said. "Whenever a gray-haired senior scientist tells you something can be done, they are almost certainly right. When they tell you it can't be done, he or she may very well be wrong," he said, referencing an adage by science fiction author Arthur C. Clarke from his famous "three laws."

"We have had a revolution in robotics, drones and warehouse robots that didn't exist. Previously, the whole thing had to be built as one huge system, an enormous thing like a aircraft carrier shipyard in space to fabricate one enormous object weighing 10,000 tonnes rather than 10 million small units each weighing a few pounds that can use mass production," he said. "We no longer need a stupendously huge factory in space and hundreds of astronauts to put it together. The whole world, other than the space program, has moved forward to mass-produced modular network devices. That's the way you would do it, and it was unthinkable 40 years ago, but suddenly it is physically, technically and economically doable."

American scientists are tinkering with the idea to this day. A group at the California Institute of Technology claims to have created a prototype that is able to capture and transmit solar energy from space, using light weight tiles, work sponsored by a $17.5 million research agreement with Northrop Grumman. Weight has always been a key issue to resolve because of the cost of rocket launches being based on weight of cargo. Thin film solar panels are lightweight, which reduces launch cost. Though as launch costs come down it may be less of a make-or-break issue. Thin film may also have a structural advantage in space—the lighter weight is no issue in the zero-gravity environment.

Other nations are exploring the concept. In India and in Europe scientists are working on additional concepts for solar based power in space. Japan's JAXA, an aerospace exploration agency, has been researching how to overcome technological barriers, such as microwave wireless power transmission tech and robotic assembly tech.

The US Military Has Begun Exploring the Idea

The most important U.S. effort underway today is arguably the one being conducted by the U.S. military, which received $178 million in its current fiscal year to explore space-based solar power.

For the military, space-based solar could solve big issues with delivering power to posts in remote locations, such as in Afghanistan, where getting fuel to a base means driving a truck loaded with flammable gasoline through hostile territory. Solar power beamed from space would also offer bases a new method of powering their operations, recharging the huge battery packs that soldiers carry today because they have so many electronic devices, and could lead to a ramp up in use more electric vehicles. "Anything the military does will push the technology, and CalTech is push-ing hard too with the thin film cells, and that work is going well," Hopkins said.

A Department of Defense spokesman said the DoD routinely conducts research to explore concepts such as space-based solar power, but it did not have details to provide at this time.

One of the concerns that has dogged the concept is the idea that these projects are really clandestine efforts to develop a space-based laser cannon. Mankins said those fears are based in real physics, but not supported by the reality of military equipment monitoring by the world's powers. High frequency lasers could be concentrated to serve as a weapon, but any equip-ment with that purpose would be obvious in its construction, and that is construc-tion that is easily monitored from the earth. "If you look at armored vehicles with machine guns versus a Ford F150 pickup, the difference would be discernible from the ground, even if there are some similarities," Mankins said. "You would see some-thing that looked like a Hubble telescope."

> **Studies conducted on feasibility are decades old and simply no longer relevant.**

Risks of Solar in Space

Hughes said that going into space and intercepting sunlight that would have oth-erwise gone past the earth can heat up the temperature within our atmosphere, though he added that this effect depend on the size of the solar collector in space.

"If the plan is to capture solar energy in space, that means the total amount of solar energy going into earth goes up, that increases the earth's temperature," Hughes said. "Now of course that depends on how much energy is being brought in. It only becomes a problem when the area of the solar connectors in space becomes comparable to the size of earth."

Mankins said there are significant risks for the planet that need to be consid-ered, including an increase in temperature and unintended consequences for vari-ous forms of life. "There is a reason birds like to sit on utility wires." But it is no dif-ferent that worries about UV rays, and the concerns are "not known showstoppers."

He said the length of microwaves being contemplated for these projects do not pose a significant health risk. He also studied the global warming argument in detail and said it is a fact that beaming power from space to the earth will have an impact on surface temperatures. But when you look at how efficient the delivery of solar from space could be versus the addition of more coal-powered, natural gas-fired or diesel power generation, the resulting greenhouse gas emissions are still much lower.

Michael Byers, a professor in the department of political science at University British Columbia Vancouver says the biggest problem for this concept may be a matter of time. Space-based systems might well be possible several decades from now, but Earth-based systems are already catching up to fossil fuels in terms of cost and efficiency. "You can put solar panels just about anywhere. Rooftops are the most obvious location, and in some jurisdictions all new buildings must have solar arrays. Lots of small projects are better than a few big ones, since they provide greater resilience to equipment failures and weather events," Byers said.

> **One thing the Chinese are really good at is thinking long-term, unlike U.S. thinking, out 50 years about this stuff. They have no problem thinking like that.**
> **Mark Hopkins**
> NATIONAL SPACE SOCIETY BOARD OF DIRECTORS

Hopkins said price competition from Earth-based utility generation is a real issue, but not an insurmountable one. As prices fall for solar technology on the ground, they fall for solar that would be used in space as well. And space-based solar—because it can beam electricity anywhere in the world—can take advantage of the big price differential in the utility market.

A space-based solar system can target places like Japan or Hawaii, where electricity prices can be four to five times prices in the mainland U.S. and then can move to lower-cost electricity markets later once the solar project has paid for itself. "That's the military thinking. The money you are sending to remote military bases can pay for the technology later. There is a return on investment in the future that doesn't require sending the electricity to Los Angeles today."

But the detractors remains convinced it is an idea that will remain in the world of Asimov's stories.

"The concept of space solar power is and will remain in the realm of science fiction for a long time, maybe forever. Even if China or any other nation decides to build an SBSP demonstrator, it does not mean that it is a good idea and that it makes economic sense to do so," L de Weck said.

National Space Society director Hopkins said that kind of thinking—coupled with the U.S. government's inability to think long-term in its planning—may be the biggest risk of all. He said that current views in the U.S. on the topic tend to fall into one of two camps.

"People in the U.S. tend to look at it as, 'At least the Chinese are doing it, and if the Chinese are doing it, then we are likely to do it at some point because we don't want them to lead.' Others are saying, 'If they get this right and we don't, we are in big trouble.'" Hopkins added, "One thing the Chinese are really good at is thinking long-term, unlike U.S. thinking, out 50 years about this stuff. They have no problem thinking like that. When I talk to NASA about anything more than 10 years out, they sort of look up in the air and roll their eyes, and I'm not invited back."

Print Citations

CMS: Rosenbaum, Eric, and Donovan Russ. "China Plans a Solar Power Play in Space That NASA Abandoned Decades Ago." In *The Reference Shelf: New Frontiers in Space,* edited by Micah L. Issitt, 24-30. Amenia, NY: Grey House Publishing, 2019.

MLA: Rosenbaum, Eric, and Donovan Russ. "China Plans a Solar Power Play in Space That NASA Abandoned Decades Ago." *The Reference Shelf: New Frontiers in Space,* edited by Micah L. Issitt, Grey Housing Publishing, 2019, pp. 24-30.

APA: Rosenbaum, E., Russ, D. (2019). China plans a solar power play in space that NASA abandoned decades ago. In Micah L. Issitt (Ed.), *The reference shelf: New frontiers in space* (pp. 24-30). Amenia, NY: Grey Housing Publishing.

2019 Is the Year That Space Tourism Finally Becomes a Reality: No, Really

By Jonathan O'Callaghan
Wired UK, January 24, 2019

Space tourism has experienced many false dawns. Companies have come and gone that have offered everything from trips to the Moon to a new home on Mars. But after broken promise after broken promise, things might be about to change.

Seven people have paid to go to space before, with American multimillionaire Dennis Tito becoming the first space tourist in 2001, flying to the International Space Station (ISS) on a Soyuz capsule to the tune of $20 million. Six more space tourists would follow in his footsteps, but despite hopes otherwise, little else followed. No space tourist has flown since 2009.

This year, however, we are expecting several private companies in the US to start taking humans to space, most for the first time. And, if all goes to plan, this could be a vital step towards making space more accessible—where paid trips and privately funded astronauts become the norm. "2019 does feel like the year that's going to be the culmination of two decades of development work that have gone into space tourism," says industry analyst Caleb Williams from consulting firm SpaceWorks. "And if we're lucky, we'll see the birth of an entirely new industry."

One of those companies is Virgin Galactic, who on 13 December 2018 conducted their first trip to near-space. Two pilots, Mark Stucky and Frederick Sturckow, took Virgin's spaceplane VSS Unity to an altitude of 82.7 kilometres (51.4 miles). This year, the company plans to conduct more test flights, with the possibility of taking its first passengers—founder Richard Branson being first of all—to space.

"We hope now to get into a regular cadence of space flights which will be historically unprecedented," says Stephen Attenborough, commercial director at Virgin Galactic. "[2019] promises to be a turning point after many years of dedication, patience and hard work."

More than 700 people have bought tickets on Virgin Galactic at a cost between $200,000 and $250,000 (£155,000 and £193,000). On each flight will be six passengers, who will experience several minutes of weightlessness and be afforded incredible views of Earth as the space plane hops into space, before returning to a runway landing.

Adventure journalist Jim Clash is one such customer, who bought ticket number 610 back in 2010. And despite the long wait, he's still as excited as ever for the flight. "Weightlessness is one thing, but I'm really going to focus on the view, trying to relax and take it all in," says Clash. "I understand that it is a life-changing experience."

> **For the moment, only the rich can afford a ticket.**

Virgin isn't the only company hoping to reach space again this year. Blue Origin, with Amazon CEO Jeff Bezos at the helm, has been making waves with its reusable New Shepard rocket , which has flown to space 10 times. Now the company is gearing up to launch humans for the first time, which may very well happen in 2019.

"We are targeting [our] first human flight this year, but we are not in a race to get there," says a spokesperson for Blue Origin. "We will move through our New Shepard flight test program step by step and fly humans only when we are ready."

Blue Origin plans to start selling tickets for its reusable rocket this year, with rumours suggesting they will charge a similar price to Virgin. Each launch, like Virgin, will also take six passengers to the edge of space. They will be free to float around the rocket's capsule for several minutes, before returning to Earth via parachute.

Also this year, we are expecting to see two private US companies—SpaceX and Boeing—begin launching astronauts to orbit. Both are contracted by NASA to take astronauts to the ISS, but the companies also plan to fly their own astronauts, a key step towards making space more accessible and opening up new doors for tourist flights. SpaceX has already begun talking about paid trips to the Moon as early as 2023.

"Space tourism has been taken much more seriously over the past several years," says space policy analyst Laura Forczyk, founder of the consulting firm Astralytical. "But once we see humans flying on commercial rockets from the US, I think that space tourism will gain credibility, and that will be great for the industry overall."

Still, for the moment only the rich can afford a ticket. It's unclear how many will be willing to do so, or how far prices will fall as the cost of flights will always be rather massive, at least in the foreseeable future. But after so many broken promises, 2019 could finally be the year that space tourism evolves from pipe dream to a reality. Four separate US companies could have launched astronauts by the year's end—and who knows what might follow.

Print Citations

CMS: O'Callaghan, Jonathan. "2019 Is the Year That Space Tourism Finally Becomes a Reality: No, Really." In *The Reference Shelf: New Frontiers in Space,* edited by Micah L. Issitt, 31-33. Amenia, NY: Grey House Publishing, 2019.

MLA: O'Callaghan, Jonathan. "2019 Is the Year That Space Tourism Finally Becomes a Reality: No, Really." *The Reference Shelf: New Frontiers in Space,* edited by Micah L. Issitt, Grey Housing Publishing, 2019, pp. 31-33.

APA: O'Callaghan, J. (2019). 2019 is the year that space tourism finally becomes a reality: No, really. In Micah L. Issitt (Ed.), *The reference shelf: New frontiers in space* (pp. 31-33). Amenia, NY: Grey Housing Publishing.

Space Solar Power: Limitless Clean Energy from Space

National Space Society, March 15, 2014 (book review)

Landmark book: The Case for Space Solar Power by John C. Mankins. A must read! This groundbreaking book by renowned expert John Mankins lays out a path forward that is both doable and affordable: within a dozen years or less, the first multi-megawatt pilot plant could be in operation. Space Solar Power could transform our future in space, and could provide a new source of virtually limitless and sustainable energy to markets across the world. See NSS review. Available as a Kindle e-book for $9.95 (with free Kindle apps for any device).

About Space Solar Power (SSP)
Also known as Space-Based Solar Power, or SBSP

The United States and the world need to find new sources of clean energy. Space Solar Power gathers energy from sunlight in space and transmits it wirelessly to Earth. Space solar power can solve our energy and greenhouse gas emissions problems. Not just help, not just take a step in the right direction, but *solve*. Space solar power can provide large quantities of energy to each and every person on Earth with very little environmental impact.

The solar energy available in space is literally billions of times greater than we use today. The lifetime of the sun is an estimated 4-5 billion years, making space solar power a truly long-term energy solution. As Earth receives only one part in 2.3 billion of the Sun's output, space solar power is by far the largest potential energy source available, dwarfing all others combined. Solar energy is routinely used on nearly all spacecraft today. This technology on a larger scale, combined with already demonstrated wireless power transmission, can supply nearly all the electrical needs of our planet.

Another need is to move away from fossil fuels for our transportation system. While electricity powers few vehicles today, hybrids will soon evolve into plug-in hybrids which can use electric energy from the grid. As batteries, super-capacitors, and fuel cells improve, the gasoline engine will gradually play a smaller and smaller role in transportation—but only if we can generate the enormous quantities of electrical energy we need. It doesn't help to remove fossil fuels from vehicles if you just turn around and use fossil fuels again to generate the electricity to power those vehicles. Space solar power can provide the needed clean power for any future electric transportation system.

While all viable energy options should be pursued with vigor, space solar power has a number of substantial advantages over other energy sources.

Advantages of Space Solar Power

- Unlike oil, gas, ethanol, and coal plants, space solar power does not emit greenhouse gases.

- Unlike coal and nuclear plants, space solar power does not compete for or depend upon increasingly scarce fresh water resources.

- Unlike bio-ethanol or bio-diesel, space solar power does not compete for increasingly valuable farm land or depend on natural-gas-derived fertilizer. Food can continue to be a major export instead of a fuel provider.

- Unlike nuclear power plants, space solar power will not produce hazardous waste, which needs to be stored and guarded for hundreds of years.

- Unlike terrestrial solar and wind power plants, space solar power is available 24 hours a day, 7 days a week, in huge quantities. It works regardless of cloud cover, daylight, or wind speed.

- Unlike nuclear power plants, space solar power does not provide easy targets for terrorists.

- Unlike coal and nuclear fuels, space solar power does not require environmentally problematic mining operations.

- Space solar power will provide true energy independence for the nations that develop it, eliminating a major source of national competition for limited Earth-based energy resources.

- Space solar power will not require dependence on unstable or hostile foreign oil providers to meet energy needs, enabling us to expend resources in other ways.

- Space solar power can be exported to virtually any place in the world, and its energy can be converted for local needs—such as manufacture of methanol for use in places like rural India where there are no electric power grids. Space solar power can also be used for desalination of sea water.

> **Space solar power can completely solve our energy problems long term.**

- Space solar power can take advantage of our current and historic investment in aerospace expertise to expand employment opportunities in solving the difficult problems of energy security and climate change.

- Space solar power can provide a market large enough to develop the low-cost space transportation system that is required for its deployment. This, in turn, will also bring the resources of the solar system within economic reach.

Disadvantages of Space Solar Power

- High development cost. Yes, space solar power development costs will be very large, although much smaller than American military presence in the Persian Gulf or the costs of global warming, climate change, or carbon sequestration. The cost of space solar power development always needs to be compared to the cost of *not*developing space solar power.

Requirements for Space Solar Power

The technologies and infrastructure required to make space solar power feasible include:

- *Low-cost, environmentally-friendly launch vehicles*. Expendable launch vehicles have been too expensive, and at high launch rates may pose atmospheric pollution problems of their own. Cheaper, reusable launch vehicles are under development by more than one private company.

- *Large scale in-orbit construction and operations*. To gather massive quantities of energy, solar power satellites must be large, far larger than the International Space Station (ISS), the largest spacecraft built to date. Fortunately, solar power satellites will be simpler than the ISS as they will consist of many identical parts.

- *Power transmission*. A relatively small effort is also necessary to assess how to best transmit power from satellites to the Earth's surface with minimal environmental impact.

All of these technologies are reasonably near-term and have multiple attractive approaches. However, a great deal of work is needed to bring them to practical fruition.

In the longer term, with sufficient investments in space infrastructure, space solar power can be built from materials from space. The full environmental benefits of space solar power derive from doing most of the work outside of Earth's biosphere. With materials extraction from the Moon or near-Earth asteroids, and space-based manufacture of components, space solar power would have essentially zero terrestrial environmental impact. Only the energy receivers need be built on Earth.

Space solar power can completely solve our energy problems long term. The sooner we start and the harder we work, the shorter "long term" will be.

Print Citations

CMS: "Space Solar Power: Limitless Clean Energy from Space." (Book review). In *The Reference Shelf: New Frontiers in Space,* edited by Micah L. Issitt, 34-37. Amenia, NY: Grey House Publishing, 2019.

MLA: "Space Solar Power: Limitless Clean Energy from Space." (Book review). *The Reference Shelf: New Frontiers in Space,* edited by Micah L. Issitt, Grey Housing Publishing, 2019, pp. 34-37.

APA: National Space Society. (2019). Space solar power: Limitless clean energy from space. (Book review). In Micah L. Issitt (Ed.), *The reference shelf: New frontiers in space* (pp. 34-37). Amenia, NY: Grey Housing Publishing.

2
The Military in Space

Pictured here is the Defense Support Program (DSP) satellite deployment during a Department of Defense space shuttle mission, STS-44. The satellite is designed to detect missile or spacecraft launches and nuclear explosions.

In Defense of Space

The recent focus on the possible creation of a new branch of the United States military devoted to space has ignited a flurry of debate among politicians and the American public alike. Is there a risk of international aggression linked to space? Should space exploration be managed internationally or through the same lens of nationalistic interest that motivates military development on Earth? These are some of the central questions in the debate over the militarization of space. Whether President Trump's ideas about space defense mark a lasting change in conservative American priorities remains to be seen, but the debate touches on many important issues in global politics.

A Military History of American Space Research

The development of space technology in the United States followed a different path from that of the former Soviet Union. While the USSR (Union of Soviet Socialist Republics) made their space program an entirely military endeavor, the United States founded the National Aeronautics and Space Administration (NASA) as a pseudo-civilian program, though heavily influenced by policy directives from the Pentagon and intelligence community. President Dwight D. Eisenhower's correspondence indicates that he pursued a cooperative relationship with Russia in the Space Race, writing letters to Prime Minister Nikolai Bulganin (in 1957) and then Premier Nikita Khrushchev (in 1958), but these offers were rejected because the United State refused to remove nuclear weapons from Turkey and other locations.

While the United States and Russia remained hostile, there was limited cooperation between space agencies in the two countries. Interestingly, the first cooperative exercise was inspired by the 1969 film *Marooned*, starring Gregory Peck and Gene Hackman, in which a fictional group of stranded U.S. astronauts are rescued by Russian cosmonauts. The film helped to inspire interest in cooperative contact in both the United States and Russia and played a role in negotiations for what became the Apollo-Soyuz Test Project of 1975, the first U.S.-Russian cooperative mission in space. In this historic event, the U.S. Apollo vehicle docked with the Russian *Soyuz* spacecraft and the astronauts and cosmonauts aboard met and shook hands in a gesture of peace. This event occurred at the height of the Cold War, even as the military-industrial complexes of both nations continued their feud through the proliferation of weapons.[1]

Limited and largely symbolic cooperative gestures continued sporadically through the 1970s and 1980s, though such efforts were closely watched by the military and intelligence communities. A new host of private space organizations, like the Planetary Society created by famed U.S. astronomer Carl Sagan and NASA's Jet Propulsion Laboratory, engaged in cooperative exchanges with Soviet scientists and frequently encouraged the view that space should be a peaceful new vista in human existence, rather than another battleground for political power struggles.

In 1983, President Ronald Reagan called for the creation of the Strategic Defense System (SDI), a space-based defense grid that would have consisted of armed satellites designed to protect the United States from an intercontinental ballistic missile attack. Reagan's proposal, though it failed to materialize, was quickly dubbed the "Star Wars" initiative after the film series.[2]

The beginning of the failed Star Wars program was also the beginning of the end of the Cold War. Reagan and then Soviet president Mikhail Gorbachev signed agreements to further scientific cooperation, though little cooperation occurred. After the United States suffered a setback to its space program when the space shuttle *Challenger* exploded in 1986, and after Russia achieved another major milestone with the launch of the six modules that composed the Mir Space Station, Russian leaders agreed to a new cooperative agreement with the United States, even if the United States could not agree to abandon the SDI program.

As history indicates, the development of U.S. space technology has always been closely linked to the goals of the nation's military industrial complex as well as to the perception of threats or competition from other nations involved in developing space technology. The Cold War fueled the space race, but also hampered development of scientific goals by reducing cooperation between global leaders in the field. Presidents elected during the Cold War frequently attempted to navigate the uncertain line between appeasing those interested in preserving or advancing the nation's military advantage and the views of the majority of the world's scientists, who saw this new era of space exploration as an opportunity to expand and renew peaceful cooperation between nations.

The Militarization of Space

In 2018, President Trump suggested that the United States needed to create a new military division charged with addressing threats from space. As Trump stated:

"When it comes to defending America, it is not enough to merely have an American presence in space. We must have American dominance in space."[3]

While some critics immediately decried this idea as misguided, the Space Force proposal is neither radical nor especially unusual given the history of American military development since the Cold War. This is an idea that has been considered by many previous presidential administrations and has been the subject of much analyses by military experts and contractors. Trump's primary contribution was to brand the idea as a "Space Force" and then to suggest that it should be its own military branch, rather than a subdivision of an existing branch. The program would constitute a massive new commercial enterprise and would require new educational facilities, bases, new technology, and new jobs for private companies.

Since the Cold War, the standard approach to military spending has been to initiate new programs, with new sources of funding, rather than continuing existing programs. Incoming presidential administrations have tended to espouse this method because doing so generates a higher level of media and public interest. The

Space Force proposal, for which Trump asked Congress to allocate $8 billion, follows this basic pattern. As of 2019, the United States spends around $649 billion annually on defense, which is the most any nation spends on defense by a wide margin. Consider that China, Saudi Arabia, India, France, Russia, the UK and Germany combined spend an annual $609 billion, and it becomes apparent how much U.S. spending on the military outpaces the rest of the world.

The Trump administration's justification for Space Force is to protect satellite systems and other space assets as well as to integrate defensive and offensive systems that could, as described in the 2018 Department of Defense report on the proposal, "degrade, deny, disrupt, destroy, and manipulate adversary capabilities." In other words, the idea of the Space Force is to protect existing commercial assets while at the same time give the United States an early advantage in the future of a militarized space environment. In 2007, China used a ballistic missile to destroy one of their own satellites, and Russia is known to have been testing missiles with the capability to destroy satellites. Such incidents have been used to prove the necessity of military space defense systems. Though the proposal for Space Force originated with the Trump administration, American military agencies have been developing military space technology for decades. Among the tools developed in this vein is the top-secret X-37B aircraft, the capabilities of which remain unknown though the Air Force has conducted experiments using the aircraft to orbit the Earth.[4]

Reaction to Trump's Space Force proposal has been mixed. Experts in the field warn that such a program is not feasible and advocate for the wealth of other space-based programs that might take precedence. America's military-industrial complex objected to the cost and to the fact that the resources would detract from more immediate programs. Writing in *Time* magazine, Jeffrey Kluger opined that "good government is often unglamorous stuff—fixing pot holes, plowing snow, collecting trash," and suggested that Trump, unsatisfied with the relative banality of addressing known problems in space, such as the accumulation of potentially dangerous "space debris," opted for a proposal he knew would be most ostentatious and bold, hoping to capture public attention. [5]

Star Trek or Star Wars

As of 2019, a compromise has been reached in which a new division of the Air Force will be created focusing on space issues rather than a unique branch of the armed forces.[6] The $8 billion in initial funding requested by Trump was rejected in favor of more modest efforts to refocus existing Air Force activities. While Trump's proposal and the controversy that followed was short-lived in the United States, it inspired debates about space militarization around the world. In 2019, it was announced that France would be investing significantly in space defense, and some reports indicated that China too was heading in that direction. However, *South China Morning Post* writer Minnie Chan reported in October 2018 that Chinese leadership was approaching the issue in a far-less reactionary way, stating, "the cold war has taught Beijing the danger of being drawn into a reckless race for supremacy."[7] Some analysts believe, however, that there is danger of a new era of weapons proliferation between the United States and China.

A number of prominent physicists and space scientists have come forward to argue that space should not be militarized but should be a free, open environment belonging equally to all mankind. Though the early history of space science was dominated by the military pressures and fears that drove the advancement of the technology, space ultimately became an arena for unprecedented cooperation, even between representatives of hostile nations, and it is this legacy of space that opponents of cosmic militarization seek to protect.

Works Used

Bacevich, Andrew J. "Op-Ed: Trump's Ridiculous Space Force Is—Sadly—an Extension of America's Existing National Security Strategy." *Los Angeles Times*. Jun 21, 2018.

Bachman, Justin, and Travis Tritten. "Why Trump Wants a Space Force for the Final Frontier." *The Washington Post*. Feb 19, 2019. Retrieved from https://www.washingtonpost.com/business/why-trump-wants-a-space-force-for-the-final-frontier/2019/02/19/aac0b1ee-349d-11e9-8375-e3dcf6b68558_story.html?noredirect=on.

Chan, Minnie. "Why Donald Trump's New Space Force Can't Hurt China Like Star Wars Hurt the Soviet Union." South China Morning Post. Oct 4, 2018. Retrieved from https://www.scmp.com/news/china/military/article/2166844/why-donald-trumps-new-space-force-cant-hurt-china-star-wars-hurt.

Glass, Andrew. "President Reagan Calls for Launching 'Star Wars' Initiative, March 23, 1983." *Politico*. Mar 23, 2017. Retrieved from https://www.politico.com/story/2017/03/president-reagan-calls-for-launching-star-wars-initiative-march-23-1983-236259.

Kluger, Jeffrey. "Why Trump's 'Space Force' Won't—and Shouldn't—Happen." *Time*. Jun 19, 2018. Retrieved from https://time.com/5316007/space-force-trump/.

Sagdeev, Roald, and Eisenhower, Susan. "United States-Soviet Space Cooperation during the Cold War." *NASA*. Retrieved from https://www.nasa.gov/50th/50th_magazine/coldWarCoOp.html.

Schlosser, Eric. "The Growing Dangers of the New Nuclear-Arms Race." *New Yorker*. May 24, 2018. Retrieved from https://www.newyorker.com/news/news-desk/the-growing-dangers-of-the-new-nuclear-arms-race.

Shieber, Jonathan. "Space Force Will Be a Marines-Like Branch under Air Force Authority." *Tech Crunch*. Retrieved from https://techcrunch.com/2019/02/19/marines-in-space/.

"The Truman Doctrine, 1947." *U.S. Department of State*. Office of the Historian. 2016. Retrieved from https://history.state.gov/milestones/1945-1952/truman-doctrine.

"U.S. Defense Spending Compared to Other Countries." *PGPF*. Peter G. Peterson Foundation. May 3, 2019. Retrieved from https://www.pgpf.org/chart-archive/0053_defense-comparison.

Notes

1. Sagdeev and Eisenhower, "United States-Soviet Space Cooperation during the Cold War."
2. Glass, "President Reagan Calls for Launching 'Star Wars' Initiative, March 23, 1983."
3. Bacevich, "Op-Ed: Trump's Ridiculous Space Force Is—Sadly—an Extension of America's Existing National Security Strategy."
4. Bachman and Tritten, "Why Trump Wants a Space Force for the Final Frontier."
5. Kluger, "Why Trump's 'Space Force' Won't—and Shouldn't—Happen."
6. Shieber, "Space Force Will Be a Marines-Like Branch under Air Force Authority."
7. Chan, "Why Donald Trump's New Space Force Can't Hurt China Like Star Wars Hurt the Soviet Union."

The Moon's Role in the New U.S. Space Force

By Paul D. Spudis

Air & Space, August 17, 2018

In a speech last week at the Pentagon, Vice President Mike Pence announced that the Trump administration is working with the Department of Defense to create the United Space Command. The Administration is asking Congress for an additional $8 billion for space security systems over the next five years, and signaling that it is ready to work with Congress to create a sixth branch of the armed forces—the U.S. Space Force.

The idea of a Space Force, first floated by the President last March, has drawn mixed reactions from politicians and left some space advocates perplexed. Do we not want to keep outer space a domain where nations peacefully gather to conduct scientific exploration and deploy services such as weather monitoring? Isn't that what the Outer Space Treaty of 1967 was all about?

In truth, space has always been a military arena. Many nations depend on sophisticated and expensive satellites to keep them informed and secure, and the satellites themselves require protection. The United States, Russia and China have all launched and tested anti-satellite weapons—interceptors that can destroy a satellite in space. China demonstrated as recently as 2007 how easily satellites could be damaged by an enemy.

At the same time, national security has been a technology driver for the U.S. space program since its inception, even before the Soviet Union's launch of Sputnik in 1957 put space in the spotlight. My lifelong interest in history and the military stems in large part from being an Army brat. During my father's military career, our family was posted at different forts around the United States and overseas. One was a special favorite of mine—Fort Huachuca, in the Huachuca Mountains of southern Arizona near the Mexican border. It was here, in the early '60s, where my father worked on the MOBIDIC—a semi-truck-sized computer, with the then-amazing capacity to address up to seven banks of 4.1K RAM memory.

Thirty years later, in my chosen career of space science, I became involved in the DoD-NASA lunar mission called Clementine. Once again, as throughout history, science and military technology enabled each other, sparking breakthroughs in both fields. Clementine was designed to test new technologies on a space-based platform, without violating any then-existing treaty restrictions. Mapping the Moon and finding polar ice—a valuable and strategic space-based asset yet to be claimed—was a bonus. Clementine's engineering model is currently on display at the National Air and Space Museum, in the Mary Baker Engen Restoration Hangar at the Steven F. Udvar-Hazy Center in suburban Washington, D.C.

Today the world's economies and militaries are more dependent than ever on space assets. And with many nations, including U.S. adversaries, rapidly improving their own space technology, American satellites are increasingly vulnerable.

Scenarios for anti-satellite warfare have mostly focused on low Earth orbit (200-500 km) and geosynchronous orbit (36,000 km), where most of our satellites are stationed. Typically in these scenarios, interceptors launched from the ground either collide with an enemy satellite or explode near it.

But now that we are planning a return to the Moon, the entire volume of cislunar space (a radius of 400,000 km) becomes a potential battleground. In 1998, a launch malfunction resulted in a very valuable Hughes communications satellite being stranded in a useless orbit. Hughes engineers ingeniously used the spacecraft's reserve attitude control fuel to gradually swing the satellite around the Moon and bring it back down to its correct orbit. The maneuver resulted in the satellite approaching Earth from an unusual, "stealthy" direction—downwards from the Moon rather than up from the ground, the way we typically think of missile launches by aggressor nations.

This "oops" event turned into an eye-opening realization for military space experts: It's very difficult to conduct surveillance on the entire volume of space beyond low Earth orbit. China also understood the implications of cislunar orbits, and in 2010 flew its Chang'E-2 scientific spacecraft to the Moon, orbited it for a year, then moved the spacecraft to a halo orbit around the Earth-Moon L-2 libration point (60,000 km above the center of the lunar far side). After loitering there for eight months, Chang'E-2 then took off for a flyby interception of the asteroid Toutatis. In a single mission, China demonstrated "space control," or the ability to place any kind of satellite—friendly or unfriendly—virtually anywhere in cislunar space.

> **With many nations, including U.S. adversaries, rapidly improving their own space technology, American satellites are increasingly vulnerable.**

Such an ability would give any nation a decided edge in a future space-based conflict. Not only does the Moon offer a gravitational rallying point for changing orbits, stealthy spacecraft could hide at the libration points of the Earth-Moon system, nearly undetectable with conventional space tracking.

It is imperative that the United States be prepared for this new theater of engagement. Building a cislunar spacefaring transportation system of the kind that I and others have advocated would put us in a position to dispatch spacecraft to any point in the Earth-Moon neighborhood, whether for science, commerce, or defense. This doesn't mean we're "militarizing" space—it already is militarized. And if the United States does not maintain a presence in and around cislunar space, it will have no leverage to protect its own satellites and those of our allies.

Fortunately, many of the requirements for guaranteeing national security in space are the same as those for setting up lunar outposts dedicated to science or commerce. An outpost focused on lunar ice harvesting—learning how to provision ourselves in space (it's prohibitively expensive to bring everything along)—would serve all three purposes simultaneously. In that sense, NASA's renewed interest in the Moon and the plan for a Space Force are in perfect harmony.

Print Citations

CMS: Spudis, Paul D. "The Moon's Role in the New U.S. Space Force." In *The Reference Shelf: New Frontiers in Space,* edited by Micah L. Issitt, 47-49. Amenia, NY: Grey House Publishing, 2019.

MLA: Spudis, Paul D. "The Moon's Role in the New U.S. Space Force." *The Reference Shelf: New Frontiers in Space,* edited by Micah L. Issitt, Grey Housing Publishing, 2019, pp. 47-49.

APA: Spudis, P.D. (2019). The Moon's role in the new U.S. space force. In Micah L. Issitt (Ed.), *The reference shelf: New frontiers in space* (pp. 47-49). Amenia, NY: Grey Housing Publishing.

Trump's Space Force Gets the Final Frontier All Wrong

By Peter Juul
Foreign Policy, March 20, 2019

Just before Valentine's Day last month, NASA made one final call to Opportunity, the little Mars rover that had been trekking across the red planet since it arrived in 2004. The space agency lost contact with the robotic explorer in June 2018 during a massive planetary dust storm and had been attempting to reconnect with it ever since. To no avail: "With a sense of deep appreciation and gratitude," NASA officials declared on February 13 that Opportunity was dead and its mission was over.

Americans from former President Barack Obama on down bid a fond farewell to what *Wired* called "the hardest-working robot in the solar system." Indeed, it had lasted almost 15 years despite being designed to have a life span of just three months. Opportunity is survived on Mars by two other American robotic explorers: fellow rover Curiosity and the recently arrived InSight lander.

Less than a week after NASA's announcement, U.S. President Donald Trump issued Space Policy Directive-4, which formally established the United States Space Force as a new branch of the U.S. military. During the Trump administration's yearlong public campaign supporting the creation of a Space Force, it repeatedly forged dangerous rhetorical links between NASA's peaceful space exploration program and the exploitation of space for U.S. national security purposes. In October 2018, for instance, Vice President Mike Pence—head of the National Space Council—claimed that a Space Force was necessary to ensure "that we have the security in space to advance human space exploration."

His bombast didn't just blur conceptual lines that ought to remain as sharp as they have been since the start of the space age in 1957. It revealed that the administration doesn't grasp the nature of American leadership on the final frontier. Space exploration has certainly been driven by geopolitical concerns, but not by the narrow and reactive security calculations propelling the Trump administration's Space Force proposal.

As the public reaction to Opportunity's demise shows, the real geopolitics of space exploration remain bound up with national pride and prestige—and not just for the United States. Just a week before Opportunity fell silent, Japan's Hayabusa 2 probe landed on the asteroid Ryugu and began taking samples to return to Earth. A few days into the new year, China's Chang'e 4 spacecraftsuccessfully alighted on the far side of the Moon. India and the European Space Agency both maintain Mars orbiters that circle the planet alongside their American counterparts. Most recently, the launch of a lunar lander built by a private Israeli nonprofit has become a focus of national pride for Israel.

More robotic explorers from even more nations are on the way: The United Arab Emirates plans to send its own probe to Mars in 2020, while Japan, China, and the European Space Agency all aim to launch complex robotic missions on the red planet and its moons over the next several years. India hopes to launch another Mars mission in the same time frame, and it appears set to send a lander and rover to the lunar surface sometime this year. For its part, South Korea intends to put a robotic explorer into lunar orbit in 2020.

This new multinational flotilla of robotic explorers sailing through the solar system shouldn't be surprising. Since the dawn of the space age, nations large and small have sought to demonstrate their technological skill and economic strength through daring feats of human and robotic spaceflight. More importantly, however, great powers have always seen space exploration as a matter of national prestige and international standing. A nation cannot be considered truly influential or powerful, it seems, unless it explores the heavens. And with relations between countries on the ground becoming more competitive, it is not surprising that the space race has picked back up too.

To be sure, today's quest for international status looks to be more friendly and productive than the Cold War competition between the Soviet Union and the United States. But it nevertheless marks a shift away from the collaborative climate that characterized the post-Cold War era—and represents an opportunity for the United States to show that it is still the standard-bearer of the future.

U.S. President John F. Kennedy made it clear that the quest for national prestige defined his space program in his famous 1962 address on America's nascent effort to put a man on the moon: "No nation which expects to be the leader of other nations can expect to stay behind in the race for space." The Apollo program would demonstrate America's superior ambition and skill to the world in spectacular fashion. Similar motives drove U.S. President Richard Nixon to approve the space shuttle program in the 1970s and U.S. President Ronald Reagan to push for a permanently inhabited space station in the 1980s.

> **Rather than embarking on a futile security competition in space through the creation of a new military service, the United States should favor peaceful exploration that brings benefits to all nations.**

The end of the Cold War marked an end to the competitive epoch of space exploration. By the late 1980s, traditional allies like Canada, Japan, and the European Space Agency had all signed on to help NASA build President Reagan's proposed space station. Presidents George W. Bush and Bill Clinton brought Russia into the project after the fall of the Soviet Union, and the construction and continued operation of the International Space Station over 20 years remains an impressive feat of global collaboration.

Today, however, the United States finds itself on the precipice of a new and uncertain era. American astronauts continue to live and work aboard the International Space Station, but no American has rocketed into orbit from U.S. territory since the last flight of the space shuttle in 2011. And back on Earth, the United States and its democratic allies in Europe and Asia have settled into a worldwide competition for power and influence with Russia and China.

Now Russia remains the only nation that regularly launches humans into space. Meanwhile, reflecting their growing power, new players like India and China have embarked on their own ambitious robotic exploration missions to Mars and the far side of the moon. National prestige and international standing are once more at the forefront of space exploration, as is competition between nations—especially between democracies and autocracies—to make impressive achievements on the final frontier.

To navigate the new space competition, the United States must first recognize that national prestige and global standing are critical national interests worth pursuing and not pointless—and possibly dangerous—chest-thumping exercises. And peaceful space exploration provides the United States a huge opportunity to restore pride at home and burnish its prestige overseas. It certainly beats other—perhaps less productive—ways of seeking international status, such as stockpiling nuclear weapons.

America starts with an advantage on this front despite not having launched astronauts from its own soil in almost eight years. Even after five decades, the Apollo moon landings continue to stir pride at home and admiration abroad. The space shuttle remains iconic nearly a decade after retirement, while the cosmic images beamed back from the Hubble Space Telescope continue to provoke awe and wonder. Astronauts aboard the International Space Station have turned their own camera lenses back toward Earth and given the world stunning images of our home planet. Robotic explorers from Voyager to the Mars rovers and New Horizons have kept the country on the cutting edge of discovery in our solar system.

But this advantage won't last forever. Without consistent and increased funding for NASA, ambitious programs of both human and robotic exploration will literally fail to leave the ground. Progress doesn't entail an Apollo-level commitment of national resources, but instead funding comparable to the early 1990s. An additional $5 billion a year should get the job done, with $3 billion for human exploration and $2 billion for robotic missions.

But funding isn't everything, and in the new geopolitical context, democracy must be seen to work effectively. When it comes to space exploration, that means ratcheting back U.S. space cooperation with Russia as well as forgoing any equally intimate cooperation with China and its secretive space agency. The fact that the head of Russia's space agency remains under U.S. sanctions for his role in Moscow's military intervention in Ukraine illustrates the hazards involved in working with autocracies in space. Deep cooperation with autocratic powers in space gives autocracies a major point of diplomatic leverage over the United States, and more generally allows them to poach unearned international prestige by working on goals set and largely carried out by the United States. In today's world, there's no reason for the United States to give Russia or China this sort of standing by association.

Cooperation between the United States and Russia won't grind to an immediate halt, though. With the International Space Station in orbit until at least 2024—if not longer—it will take time to disentangle the web of functional ties that have bound NASA and its Russian counterpart over the last quarter century. Significant cooperation with China should be avoided altogether, especially given its notoriously opaque and military-run space program. The space programs and agencies of other nations—NASA, the European Space Agency and its member-nation agencies, the Japan Aerospace Exploration Agency, and even Russia's Roscosmos—remain led and run by civilians.

In the meantime, the United States should buttress its already strong cooperative ties with fellow democracies like Japan, Canada, and the nations of the European Space Agency. Here, the main diplomatic challenge with partners like the ESA will be to convince them to curb their enthusiasm for cooperation with Russia and China on space exploration. The United States should also forge stronger space ties with interested democratic allies like South Korea, as well as newcomers like India and Israel.

Above all, the United States should foster an atmosphere of productive competition when it comes to space exploration. It should serve as a spur to achievement rather than animosity, as nations strive to outdo one another on the final frontier. In other words, rather than embarking on a futile security competition in space through the creation of a new military service, the United States should favor peaceful exploration that brings benefits to all nations. As it has since the space age began, the United States can play a pivotal leadership role in this new age of exploration.

In practical terms, all this will entail a more ambitious program of human and robotic exploration than is currently under consideration. When it comes to human spaceflight, the country should continue to focus on a voyage to Mars rather than return trips to the lunar surface. For robotic missions, NASA should opt for technically demanding projects that concentrate on the outer solar system—the moons of Jupiter or an ice giant planet like Neptune, for instance—in addition to enduring priorities like Martian exploration.

The resources NASA devotes to research and development will pull the American technology sector in new, unexpected, and innovative directions. NASA's engagement with the United States' leading tech and aerospace companies, moreover, gives the country a critical advantage that doesn't exist in the world of autocracies.

Concerns about national prestige and international status will always be an essential part of global politics. But not all prestige projects are created equal, and few offer as wide a suite of benefits as space exploration: investment in cutting-edge domestic industries, technological innovation, the creation of communities of engineering expertise, and, of course, scientific discovery. More than that, though, space exploration points the way to a more hopeful future—both for the nations that participate and for humanity.

At a time of increased geopolitical competition between democracies and autocracies, the United States should do its utmost to maintain its standing as the world's leading spacefaring nation. America possesses a space exploration advantage too valuable to throw away through lack of investment or the pursuit of a militarized approach to space. This high ground gives the United States the ability to set the terms of the next geopolitical era of space exploration—and it should seize the opportunity to foster a spirit of friendly and productive competition.

The United States can win this competition—and in today's geopolitical world, it's one the country cannot afford to lose.

Print Citations

CMS: Juul, Peter. "Trump's Space Force Gets the Final Frontier All Wrong." In *The Reference Shelf: New Frontiers in Space,* edited by Micah L. Issitt, 50-54. Amenia, NY: Grey House Publishing, 2019.

MLA: Juul, Peter. "Trump's Space Force Gets the Final Frontier All Wrong." *The Reference Shelf: New Frontiers in Space,* edited by Micah L. Issitt, Grey Housing Publishing, 2019, pp. 50-54.

APA: Juul, P. (2019). Trump's space force gets the final frontier all wrong." In Micah L. Issitt (Ed.), *The reference shelf: New frontiers in space* (pp. 50-54). Amenia, NY: Grey Housing Publishing.

A Handshake in Space Changed US-Russia Relations: How Long Will It Last?

By Monica Grady

The Conversation, July 17, 2015

Exactly 40 years ago, a historic handshake took place between Russian cosmonaut Aleksey Leonov and US astronaut Tom Stafford during a joint USSR-American docking mission, kicking off a successful collaboration between the two countries in space. That cooperation has lasted, even when relationships on the ground deteriorated. But now that there are more international entrants in the field of space exploration, how firm will the US-Russia bond hold, especially as political tensions rise?

For now, however, US and Russia are working together. Some 400 km above us, the International Space Station (ISS) is orbiting with three crew members on board: two Russians and one American. Next week, a rocket launched from the Russian launch facility in Baikonur, Kazakhstan, will carry a Japanese astronaut, plus a third Russian and a second American.

The crew of six will work together until just before Christmas, when they will return to Earth. The ISS is a great example of how international relations should work, and is an active manifestation of the Global Space Exploration Strategy, established in 2007. This is a roadmap for robotic and human exploration of space, endorsed by 14 separate space agencies, including NASA, the European Space Agency and the Russian, Japanese and Chinese counterparts.

From Competition to Co-dependency

This is a very different picture of space exploration from 50 years ago, when the USA and the USSR were firmly gripped in a Cold War and a space race. In 1965, the USA was lagging behind the Soviet competition. Still smarting from losing out to Sputnik (the first artificial satellite, launched in 1957), Yuri Gagarin (first man in space, 1961) and Valentina Tereshkova (first woman in space, 1963), America focused its efforts on sending a man to the moon.

Part of the drive behind the space race was its mirroring of poor international relations between the US and USSR superpowers. While not actively engaged in direct conflict, the Cold War, the Cuban Missile crisis and war in Vietnam all provided opportunities for tension between the two nations. How, then, did we move from international competition to collaboration?

It only took a decade for matters to change dramatically. By 1975, the US had gained international accolades for the achievements of the Apollo astronauts, and was leading the world in exploration of other planets. In contrast, the USSR had had more limited success with its series of probes to Venus and Mars, and was concentrating much of its efforts on its Salyut programme of Earth orbiters and long duration flights.

Although international relations between the superpowers were still frosty, there was an easing in dialogue brought about by mutual visits by the presidents of each country. Threat of nuclear war was diminished following signing of the Strategic Arms Limitation Treaty (SALT), and trading embargoes were lifted.

The handshake between Stafford and Leonov, televised across the globe, was one of the major symbols of the new détente between America and USSR. It started with a bit of to-ing and fro-ing, a quick eye contact, then a handshake. But the overwhelming significance was where this took place: 230 km above the Earth's surface.

> One development that could put an end to these uncertainties is the rise of private companies involved in space exploration.

Leonov, the Russian Commander, was an experienced cosmonaut, the first man to undertake a space walk. Stafford, the US Commander, had been Commander of Apollo 10, which all but landed on the Moon. The two men spoke in Russian and English, and exchanged flags. It meant that, not quite 20 years after it had begun, the space race had officially come to an end and an era of four decades of close collaboration in space would follow.

Trouble on the Horizon?

In the last few years, however, the political situation has been getting more fraught as Russia continues its conflict with Ukraine. While scientists are hoping this won't affect the space exploration relationship, this is not something that can be taken for granted. In response to sanctions from the US, Russia's deputy prime minister Dmitry Rogozin said in 2014 that the country would reject a US request to extend the use of the ISS beyond 2020.

In February this year, however, Russia agreed to remain part of the ISS until 2024, before setting up its own space station. But just a month later, Russian sources reported that Russia and the US had made plans to build a new joint space station after the ISS—something that the US never confirmed.

Exactly what is going to happen is hard to say but the stakes are high. Although the ISS is an international facility, it is reliant on the Russian Soyuz system to deliver and collect astronauts. Russia, however, has suffered a series of launch failures in recent years, prompting concerns that its space industry may be struggling At the same time, the end of NASA's Space Shuttle Programme, and delay of its successor, the Orion Crewed Vehicle, has meant that the US no longer has the capacity to launch people into space.

However one development that could put an end to these uncertainties is the rise of private companies involved in space exploration. Commercial companies have already been awarded contracts to supply the ISS—but not (yet) to carry astronauts.

Another significant change in recent years are the new entries into the human spaceflight business: ESA has had an astronaut training programme for many years, and is a major partner in the ISS. But it, too, is dependent on Russia for astronaut transport.

While it is hoped that the US and Russia continue their successful partnership in space, they are eventually going to have to make room for several other players. The biggest new independent player at the table is China, rapidly making great strides in progress, following the successful launch of the first 'taikonaut' in 2003.

In the same way that, in the past USSR kept many of its space technology developments (and failures) secret, China tends not to announce its plans ahead of the game, so it is possible that China might be building the capacity to establish a more permanent base in orbit around the Earth. As of now, because of security concerns, NASA researchers are not allowed to work with Chinese citizens affiliated with a Chinese state organisation. This has prevented Chinese astronauts visiting the ISS, and is regretted.

In recent years, despite political upheavals, changes in administrations and realignment of national space priorities, there has been a great deal of international good will towards the ISS. This is as much because of what it stands for, as what it does. The ISS is a clear representation that human spaceflight has to be co-operative and that no single nation can go it alone.

As larger numbers of countries become involved in space exploration, the ISS, representing as it does the "final frontier," could act as a buffer zone from international politics, where confrontation once again gives way before handshakes between colleagues.

Print Citations

CMS: Grady, Monica. "A Handshake in Space Changed US-Russia Relations: How Long Will It Last?" In *The Reference Shelf: New Frontiers in Space,* edited by Micah L. Issitt, 55-57. Amenia, NY: Grey House Publishing, 2019.

MLA: Grady, Monica. "A Handshake in Space Changed US-Russia Relations: How Long Will It Last?" *The Reference Shelf: New Frontiers in Space,* edited by Micah L. Issitt, Grey Housing Publishing, 2019, pp. 55-57.

APA: Grady, M. (2019). A handshake in space changed US-Russia relations: How long will it last? In Micah L. Issitt (Ed.), *The reference shelf: New frontiers in space* (pp. 55-57). Amenia, NY: Grey Housing Publishing.

The U.S. Military Has Been in Space from the Beginning

By Jason Daley

The Smithsonian, June 19, 2018

The words "Space Force" conjure up images of plastoid-alloy-clad soldiers firing ray guns at aliens, but military activities in space aren't just science fiction. The U.S. military has been involved with space since the beginning, just, perhaps, not under that name.

Today, Vice President Mike Pence revealed that the administration hopes to have Space Force ready to fly by 2020 during a speech at the Pentagon. The proposal still needs congressional approval, but White House officials have steadily been pushing forward without the support of Congress. Initial moves to establish a U.S. Space Command (a combatant unit dedicated to defending space) could start by the end of the year. That would require pulling space experts from across all branches of the military and creating an office dedicated to developing space weapons and acquiring satellites. Pence also announced a new civilian position, Assistant Secretary of Defense for Space, that would oversee the establishment of the Space Force.

In June, during a meeting of the National Space Council at the White House, President Donald Trump spoke on the subject. "My administration is reclaiming America's heritage as the world's greatest space-faring nation. The essence of the American character is to explore new horizons and to tame new frontiers. But our destiny, beyond the Earth, is not only a matter of national identity, but a matter of national security," he announced. "[I]t is not enough to merely have an American presence in space. We must have American dominance in space."

Yet if the idea is to ensure the military is involved in space, a dedicated space force may not be needed; the military has been in space since space was a place you could be in. As early as 1915, the newly established National Advisory Committee for Aeronautics (NACA) was dominated by military personnel and industry executives. NACA laboratories helped develop many technologies that ended up in military aircraft during World War II. After that, NACA worked with the Air Force to develop planes capable of supersonic flight. It then moved on to working on ballistic missile designs and in the 1950s began developing plans for manned flight. In 1958, a year after the U.S.S.R's launch of the first ballistic missile and Sputnik satellite kickstarted the Space Race, NACA was rolled into the newly created NASA, a civilian agency which had a broader mandate, more power and more resources.

Clinton Parks at Space.com reports that the civilian nature of NASA was never a given. Senate Majority Leader Lyndon Johnson wanted to establish a space agency to make sure the

> **The military seems resistant to the idea of separating out a Space Force from the Air Force.**

United States controlled space militarily. President Eisenhower didn't want a space agency at all, believing it was a waste of money. Eventually, the two compromised, creating a civilian agency after Johnson was convinced space wasn't just a potential battlefield, but that a platform for scientific and technological advancement that would be a huge boon for the U.S. and commercial interests.

The establishment of NASA did not mean an end for the U.S. military in space, though many of its projects among the stars were and still are classified. In fact, during the 1960s, the U.S. Air Force ran a parallel manned space program to the one run by NASA, even designing an orbiting "laboratory" and selecting a class of 17 astronauts. Though it ran for six years, the program was cancelled in 1969 and no Air Force astronauts were launched (that we know of).

In 1982, the Air Force Space Command was officially established, and today employs 35,000 people. The agency works on cybersecurity, launches satellites and other payloads for the military and other government agencies, monitors ballistic missile launches and orbiting satellites and runs a military GPS system. And of course there's plenty of things they do that we don't know about. For instance, it's well documented that the Air Force has two X-37B space planes, including one that returned to Earth last year after two years in orbit, though what it was doing is unknown.

And NASA and the military also maintain a strong relationship. Over the decades, the vast majority of NASA astronauts have been military service members. During the heyday of the space shuttle, NASA would routinely ferry classified payloads into orbit for the Department of Defense among other projects the agencies have collaborated on.

As for the President's directive to create a new space force, Alex Ward at *Vox* reports that it may not be valid. Constitutionally, only Congress has the authority to "raise and support armies." The last branch to be created, the Air Force, was created by an act of Congress in 1947. Todd Harrison, director of the aerospace security project at the Center for Strategic and International Studies tells Patrick Kelley at *Roll Call* that "[t]he President can't create a new military service on his own. There's going to have to be legislation."

What's more, the military seems resistant to the idea of separating out a Space Force from the Air Force. Secretary of Defense Jim Mattis, for one, has gone on the record opposing the creation of a space force. Last summer, when a Space Corps proposal was floated in Congress, Mattis wrote in a letter that it would add an "additional organizational and administrative tail" and excess layers of bureaucracy to military operations. At the that time, the White House also called the establishment of a space branch "premature." Officials from the Air Force also went on record saying the move would add costs and unnecessary

That's not to say the U.S. military isn't focusing on potential threats in space. Military analyst Lt. Col. Rick Francona tells Euan McKirdy at CNN that military leaders definitely have an eye on the sky. "I hate the term 'the final frontier' but (space) is the ultimate high ground. Space doesn't dominate one small geographic area—it dominates continents, oceans," he says. "Most military thinkers know this is the battle space of the future."

Deborah Lee James, Air Force secretary during the Obama administration, agrees, pointing out that many critical satellites and communications devices necessary for modern warfare are located in space, and that other nations, China and Russia in particular, are making moves to control the region around Earth. "Space is no longer a peaceful domain," she told Ward last July. "There is a real possibility that a conflict on Earth could bleed into space."

Print Citations

CMS: Daley, Jason. "The U.S. Military Has Been in Space from the Beginning." In *The Reference Shelf: New Frontiers in Space,* edited by Micah L. Issitt, 58-60. Amenia, NY: Grey House Publishing, 2019.

MLA: Daley, Jason. "The U.S. Military Has Been in Space from the Beginning." *The Reference Shelf: New Frontiers in Space,* edited by Micah L. Issitt, Grey Housing Publishing, 2019, pp. 58-60.

APA: Daley, J. (2019). The U.S. military has been in space from the beginning. In Micah L. Issitt (Ed.), *The reference shelf: New frontiers in space* (pp. 58-60). Amenia, NY: Grey Housing Publishing.

Space Force or Space Corps?

By Kaitlyn Johnson

Center for Strategic & International Studies, June 27, 2019

The Issue

In 2018, President Trump requested that the U.S. military restructure its space offices and personnel to create a U.S. Space Force. Since then three competing visions for how the Department of Defense (DoD) should be restructured to better support its national security space enterprise have been crafted: one from the DoD itself and two from either chamber of Congress. This brief compares these three legislative proposals to create a new military service for space.

While not a new concept, the creation of a separate military service for space has gained significant momentum over the past few months. On February 28, 2019, the Department of Defense (DoD) submitted to Congress a legislative proposal to create a new military service for space within the Department of the Air Force called the United States Space Force. Initially Congress was lukewarm on the idea, but the relevant committees took up the issue and held public hearings and private meetings with officials, military professionals, and outside experts to discuss the concept.

In May and June 2019, the Senate and the House Armed Services Committees (SASC and HASC, respectively) passed military space reorganization language in their versions of the fiscal year (FY) 2020 National Defense Authorization Act (NDAA). Both committees address the issue in similar ways, yet with a few key differences.

Principally, the SASC markup is much more detailed on the requirements for the new Space Force. Arguably, the legislative proposal from DoD could be construed as a "blank check," causing the committee to add several reporting requirements and clear structural language. However, there is a key missing item despite SASC's detailed structural language: the actual declaration of a new service being created. The SASC markup never explicitly declares the establishment of a new service of the U.S. military, although it is clearly implied. The current language solely renames the existing Air Force Space Command—the primary organization that houses space personnel and capabilities within the Air Force—to the U.S. Space Force.

The HASC language creating a new military service for space did not make it into the chairman's mark of the NDAA, but it was added as an amendment to the legislation during the full committee markup. The bipartisan amendment came from congressmen, Jim Cooper (D-TN) and Mike Rogers (R-AL), who proposed a Space Corps in 2017. Unsurprisingly, the amendment looks very similar to the 2017 language that passed the full House but was later taken out in conference. The HASC version places strong emphasis on both career-building within the Space Corps and budget reporting requirements.

The most obvious difference between the SASC and HASC legislation is the name of the new service. SASC supports the name championed by President Donald Trump, the U.S. Space Force, while the HASC calls it the U.S. Space Corps. However, both envision the organization as a corps-like structure within the Department of the Air Force and a co-equal service to the U.S. Air Force. Neither supports elevating the organization to an independent military department, which is what President Trump originally suggested in June 2018.[1]

Unlike the DoD proposal, both SASC and HASC did not include a new top civilian position within the Air Force for space. This is in line with how the Marine Corps is currently structured—with the Commandant of the Marine Corps reporting directly to the secretary of the Navy. Both the SASC and HASC legislation propose a similar structure. Also similar to the Marine Corps, both the SASC and HASC propose that the new space service be led by a four-star military leader, al-

> **Three competing visions for how the Department of Defense (DoD) should be restructured to better support its national security space enterprise have been crafted.**

though the names of this new position differ. The administration proposal called the head of the Space Force a chief of staff, while the SASC calls it a commander and the HASC calls it a commandant. The SASC markup also creates a four-star vice commander position, replicating the Marine Corps' model, while the HASC makes no mention of a vice commandant position.

All three legislative proposals add the four-star in charge of the new military service to the Joint Chiefs of Staff (JCS). Both DoD's and HASC's language immediately adds the head of the space service as a representative to the JCS. The SASC markup language, however, defers the new commander to an invite-only role for the first year. The language states "upon the request of the Chairman of the Joint Chiefs of Staff, the Commander of the United States Space Force may participate in any meeting… of an issue in connection with a duty or responsibility of the Commander."[2] After the first year, however, the commander would become a full member of the JCS.

The relationship between the Space Force and U.S. Space Command (SPACE-COM) also stands out in the SASC legislation by requiring the commander of SPACECOM, likely to be Gen. John Raymond, to also act as the commander of the Space Force for the first year. After a year's time, it requires that the positions be separated.[3]

All three proposals (DoD, SASC, and HASC) make clear that the National Reconnaissance Office (NRO) will not be included in the new military service. While the fate of the NRO is unanimous, the fate of Army and Navy space operations are not. DoD's proposal included space-related personnel and operations from both the Army and Navy, although it deferred specifying which specific organizations would transfer. The HASC amendment walked that back slightly by not including the Army and Navy at the outset, but requiring the Secretary of Defense to later report to Congress "plans for the transfer or reassignment of military personnel from the space elements of the Armed Forces to the Space Corps."[4] SASC's proposal outrightly states that only personnel and operations currently belonging to the Air Force will be included in their version of the U.S. Space Force.

Markedly different in the SASC proposal is the elevation of the current principal assistant to the secretary of the Air Force for space to a principal assistant for space acquisition and integration. This new position will coordinate space acquisition efforts by overseeing the Space and Missile Systems Center (SMC), the Space Rapid Capabilities Office (Space RCO), and the new Space Development Agency (SDA). The apparent intent is to coordinate across all space acquisitions and speed decision making processes. In addition, the SASC legislation creates a Space Force Acquisition Council comprised of:

- The Under Secretary of the Air Force;

- The Principal Assistant to the Secretary of the Air Force for Space Acquisition and Integration;

- The Assistant Secretary of Defense for Space Policy;

- The Director of the National Reconnaissance Office (NRO);

- The Commander of the United States Space Command; and

- The Commander of the United States Space Force.

The purpose of the council is to oversee and coordinate space acquisitions amongst all aspects of the national security space enterprise.

While there is much to deliberate in conference, the two Congressional proposals are structurally similar, and it is likely that military space reorganization will be placed in the final version of the FY 2020 NDAA.

1 Katie Rogers, "Trump Orders Establishment of Space Force as Sixth Military Branch," *New York Times*, June 18, 2018, https://www.nytimes.com/2018/06/18/us/politics/trump-space-force-sixth-military-branch.html.

[2] U.S. Senate Armed Services Committee, "National Defense Authorization Act for Fiscal Year 2020," 116th Cong., 1st sess., 2019, S. 1790, 630, https://aerospace.csis.org/wp-content/uploads/2019/06/FY20_SASC_SpaceForce.pdf.

3 U.S. Congress, Senate, Armed Services Committee, *Nominations— Scolese,—Raymond*, 116th Cong., 1st sess., (June 4, 2019), https://www.armed-services.senate.gov/hearings/19-06-04-nominations_--scolese---raymond.

[4] U.S. House of Representatives Armed Services Committee, "National Defense Authorization Act for Fiscal Year 2020: Amendment to H.R. 2500," 116th Cong., 1st sess., 2019, H.R. 2500, 9, https://aerospace.csis.org/fy20_spacecorps_cooper-amendment/.

Print Citations

CMS: Johnson, Kaitlyn. "Space Force or Space Corps?" In *The Reference Shelf: New Frontiers in Space,* edited by Micah L. Issitt, 61-64. Amenia, NY: Grey House Publishing, 2019.

MLA: Johnson, Kaitlyn. "Space Force or Space Corps?" *The Reference Shelf: New Frontiers in Space,* edited by Micah L. Issitt, Grey Housing Publishing, 2019, pp. 61-64.

APA: Johnson, K. (2019). Space force or space corps? In Micah L. Issitt (Ed.), *The reference shelf: New frontiers in space* (pp. 61-64). Amenia, NY: Grey Housing Publishing.

Renewed Space Rivalry between Nations Ignores a Tradition of Cooperation

By Scott Shackelford

The Conversation, January 10, 2019

The annals of science fiction are full of visions of the future. Some are techno-utopian like *Star Trek* in which humanity has joined together in peace to explore the cosmos. Others are dystopian, like the World State in *Brave New World*. But many of these stories share one thing in common—they envision a time in which humanity has moved past narrow ideas of tribe and nationalism. That assumption might be wrong.

This can be seen in Trump's calls for a unified U.S. Space Command. Or, in China's expansive view of sovereignty and increasingly active space program as seen in its recent lunar landing. These examples suggest that the notion of outer space as a final frontier free from national appropriation is questionable. Active debate is ongoing as of this writing as to the consistency of the 2015 Space Act with international space law, which permitted private firms to own natural resources mined from asteroids. Some factions in Congress would like to go further still with one bill, the American Space Commerce Free Enterprise Act. This states, "Notwithstanding any other provision of law, outer space shall not be considered a global commons." This trend, especially among the space powers, is important since it not only will create precedents that could resonate for decades to come, but also because it hinders our ability to address common challenges—like removing the debris orbiting the planet.

End of the Golden Age

In 1959, then-Sen. Lyndon Johnson stated, "Men who have worked together to reach the stars are not likely to descend together into the depths of war and desolation." In this spirit, between 1962 and 1979 the United States and the former Soviet Union worked together and through the U.N. Committee for the Peaceful Uses of Outer Space to enact five major international treaties and numerous bilateral and multilateral agreements concerning outer space.

These accords covered everything from the return of rescued astronauts and liability for damage from space objects to the peaceful use of outer space. They did not, though, address space weaponization outside of the weapons of mass destruction context, or put into place mechanisms for managing an increasingly crowded final frontier.

Progress ground to a halt when it came time to decide on the legal status of the moon. The Reagan administration objected to the Moon Treaty, which stated that the moon was the "common heritage of mankind" like the deep seabed, in part because of lobbying from groups opposed to the treaty's provisions. Because no organized effort arose in support of the treaty, it died in the U.S. Senate, and with it the golden age of space law. Today, nearly 30 years after it was first proposed, only 18 nations have ratified the accord.

Rise of Collective Action Problems

Since the breakup of the Soviet Union space governance has only gotten more complicated due to an increasing number of space powers, both public and private. National and commercial interests are increasingly tied to space in political, economic and military arenas. Beyond fanciful notions of solar energy satellites, fusion energy and orbiting hotels, contemporary political issues such as nuclear nonproliferation, economic development, cybersecurity and human rights are also intimately tied to outer space.

The list of leading space powers has expanded beyond the U.S. and Russia to include China, India, Japan and members of the European Space Agency—especially France, Germany and Italy. Each regularly spends over US$1 billion on their space programs, with estimates of China's space spending surpassing $8 billion in 2017, though the U.S. continues to spend more than all other nations combined on space related efforts. But space has become important to every nation that relies on everything from weather forecasting to satellite telecommunications. By 2015, the global space industry was worth more than $320 billion, a figure that is expected to grow to $1.1 trillion by 2040.

Private companies, such as SpaceX, are working to dramatically lower the cost of launching payloads into low Earth orbit, which has long stood at approximately $10,000 per pound. Such innovation holds the promise of opening up space to new development. It also raises concerns over the sustainability of space operations.

At the same time, the Trump administration's public desire to launch a Space Force has fueled concerns over a new arms race, which, if created, could exacerbate both the issues of space weapons and debris. The two issues are related since the use of weapons in space can increase the amount of debris through fragments from destroyed satellites. For example, China performed a successful anti-satellite test in 2007 that destroyed an aging weather satellite at an altitude of some 500 miles. This single event contributed more than 35,000 pieces of orbital debris boosting the amount of space junk by approximately 25 percent.

Without concerted action, Marshall Kaplan, an orbital debris expert within the Space Policy Department at Johns Hopkins University, argues, "There is a good chance that we may have to eventually abandon all active satellites in currently used orbits" due to the growing problem of space junk.

Avoiding a Tragedy of the Space Commons

The tragedy of the commons scenario refers to the "unconstrained consumption of a shared resource—a pasture, a highway, a server—by individuals acting in rational pursuit of their self-interest," according to commons governance expert Brett Frischmann. This can and often does lead to destruction of the resource. Given that space is largely an open-access system, the pre-

> We should think long and hard before moving away from a tried and tested model like the International Space Station.

dictions of the tragedy of the commons are self-evident. Space law expert Robert Bird, has argued that nations treat orbital space as a kind of communal pasture that may be over-exploited and polluted through debris. It's a scenario captured in the movie *Wall-E*.

But luckily, there is a way out of this scenario besides either nationalization or privatization. Scholars led by the political economist and Nobel laureate Elinor Ostrom modified the tragedy of the commons by showing that, in some cases, groups can and do self-organize and cooperate to avoid tragic over exploitation.

I explore this literature on "polycentric" governance—complex governance systems made up of multiple scales, sectors and stakeholders—in my forthcoming book, *Governing New Frontiers in the Information Age: Toward Cyber Peace*. Already, we are seeing some evidence of the benefits of such a polycentric approach in an increasingly multipolar era in which there are more and more power centers emerging around the world. One example is a code of conduct for space-faring nations. That code includes the need to reduce orbital debris. Further progress could be made by building on the success of the international coalition that built the International Space Station such as by deepening partnerships with firms like SpaceX and Blue Origin.

This is not a "keep it simple, stupid" response to the challenges in space governance. But it does recognize the reality of continued national control over space operations for the foreseeable future, and indeed there are some benefits to such an outcome, including accountability. But we should think long and hard before moving away from a tried and tested model like the International Space Station and toward a future of vying national research stations and even military outposts in space.

Coordination between sovereign nations is possible, as was shown in the golden age of space law. By finding common ground, including the importance of sustainable development, we earthlings can ensure that humanity's development of space is less a race than a peaceful march—not a flags and footprints mission for one nation, but a destination serving the development of science, the economy and the betterment of international relations.

Print Citations

CMS: Shackelford, Scott. "Renewed Space Rivalry between Nations Ignores a Tradition of Cooperation." In *The Reference Shelf: New Frontiers in Space,* edited by Micah L. Issitt, 65-68. Amenia, NY: Grey House Publishing, 2019.

MLA: Shackelford, Scott. "Renewed Space Rivalry between Nations Ignores a Tradition of Cooperation." *The Reference Shelf: New Frontiers in Space,* edited by Micah L. Issitt, Grey Housing Publishing, 2019, pp. 65-68.

APA: Shackelford, S. (2019). Renewed space rivalry between nations ignores a tradition of cooperation. In Micah L. Issitt (Ed.), *The reference shelf: New frontiers in space* (pp. 65-68). Amenia, NY: Grey Housing Publishing.

Trump's Space Force Isn't the Only Military Space Program: Here's What China and Russia Are Up To

By Kyle Mizokami

Jalopnik, **February 25, 2019**

The United States may or may not be getting a Space Force, but while President Trump is all-in on the creation of a new branch of the U.S. Military—and blowing up the military bureaucracy—it's worth keeping in mind other countries have their military space programs. A recent DIA report shines a light on how the U.S. views these programs, particularly those of Russia and China, neither of which seem particularly threatening—for now anyway.

This week President Donald Trump signed Space Policy Directive 4, ordering the Pentagon to stand up the Space Force as a new branch of the U.S. military. The Space Force, which still requires the blessing of Congress, is miles from being able to put moon boots on the ground, and its existence—let alone usefulness—is still a puzzle to many. To look at how supporters justify the Space Force, it's useful to look at America's potential adversaries, particularly Russia and China, and what the U.S. government claims they're doing in space.

Russia is potentially America's foremost space adversary, at least for now anyway. Russia's space establishment is an inheritance from the Cold War-era USSR, and the country has a lot of operational extraterrestrial hardware today. The USSR never landed astronauts on the moon or flew a reusable spacecraft like the Space Shuttle, but it was the first country to put a man in space (and unlike the United States, Russia can still do that today) and orbited the space station *Mir* long before the International Space Station was in the sky.

The USSR was also arguably the first to militarize space, placing a cannon the Salyut-3 space station, and the Pentagon is still wary of Russia's intentions. The Pentagon is most concerned with Russia's military counter-space program, which it believes is pointed squarely at the United States. The Defense Intelligence Agency's Challenges to Security in Space report, published in February 2019, claims that "Russia views America's perceived dependence on space as the 'Achilles heel' of U.S. military power, which can be exploited to achieve Russian conflict objectives."

It goes on:

Russia is therefore pursuing counterspace systems to neutralize or deny U.S. space-based services, both military and commercial, as a means of offsetting a perceived U.S. military advantage and is developing an array of weapons designed to interfere with or destroy an adversary's satellites.

How does Russia plan to do this? First, Moscow needs to know what U.S. space assets to target in wartime. Despite the loss of the economic and military power of the wider Soviet Union, Russia still maintains a network of "telescopes, radars, and other sensors," capable of detecting and tracking U.S. satellites and other space objects. Russia would likely go after America's military-controlled NAVSTAR GPS satellites (24 of them), Milstar military communications satellites (eight), the Defense Satellite Communications System satellites (seven), and literally dozens of early missile warning, reconnaissance, and surveillance satellites. The loss of GPS satellites in particular would hit civilian smartphone and other GPS users around the globe.

Interfering with space assets doesn't necessarily require going into space. Moscow has led efforts to develop GPS jamming technology like something recently detected in the Black Sea and near the Russian-Norwegian border. It could also jam-interfere with satellites and their ability to pass messages between terrestrial forces. Finally, hacking satellites or ground stations could prevent their use by adversaries. Not only do none of these measures actually involve going into space, in some cases they can be done from the comfort of home.

A straightforward solution is to fire a ground-based laser at a satellite in low earth orbit, blinding or otherwise disabling it. The new DIA report warns that the Peresvet laser weapon, deployed in late 2018, is designed to attack enemy satellites. The DIA also reports that Russia is likely testing a "ground-based, mobile missile system" for the destruction of incoming ballistic missiles and satellites.

China is the other major space power. China launched its first satellite in April 1970, but ramped up space activities in the late 1990s and 2000s as the country experienced rapid economic growth. China launched its first *taikonaut*, Yang Liwei, into space in 2003, and in January 2019 landed a probe on the far side of the moon.

Like Russia, the U.S. is worried about Chinese counterspace activities potentially aimed at American satellites. Like Russia, China has a network of space surveillance assets, including telescopes, radars, and space tracking ships such as the small fleet of *Yuan Wang* space event ships, whose huge two huge high frequency parabolic antennas and optical tracking stations can monitor satellites in space.

The Defense Intelligence Agency believes that China is following a similar track to Russia, developing counterspace assets that can cripple U.S. forces in wartime. The DIA believes that China will attempt to interfere with satellites from the ground, but also believes it is prepared to physically go after satellites: Chinese research into satellites that can close with objects in space, repair satellites, and clean up "space debris," the DIA argues, could be used to go after perfectly good enemy satellites and disable them.

China also has an anti-satellite missile, the SC-19, believed to be currently operational. The SC-19 was tested in 2007 against the obsolete Fengyun-1C weather satellite, an incident viewed with alarm not just because it was an anti-satellite weapon but because it produced more than 3,000 pieces of hazardous space debris. The Pentagon believes China is developing ground-based anti-satellite weapons, including a laser that could damage the optics of spy satellites by 2020, and further in the future, a more powerful laser to disable GPS and communications satellites.

Russian and Chinese counterspace efforts are just one part of the military space efforts of both countries, but both seem pretty squarely aimed at the United States' military space assets. They are not, for example, working to place nuclear or other weapons in space that could be dropped down on the heads of ordinary Americans. Both countries realize a key truth about the modern American way of war: if war comes, America fights its wars in some else's backyard. In the event of war, U.S. forces would use communications and navigation satellites to coordinate the flow of ships, aircraft, and formations of troops over thousands of miles, across the Atlantic and Pacific Oceans to the doorsteps

> **The Space Force is still miles from being able to put moon boots on the ground, and its existence, let alone usefulness, is still a puzzle to many.**

of both Russia and China. Advocates of the U.S. Space Force believe that Russia, China, and other entities are seeking ways to disrupt that flow in wartime and give themselves an edge. That's a pretty natural reaction to a potential adversary.

There are unknowns here that should give us pause. We don't how true claims of Russian and Chinese ground-based anti-satellite lasers are. The Pentagon first warned of a similar Soviet laser weapon in 1985 but the actual system fell far short of weapon status. Another thing we don't know: the intent of Russia and China to use anti-satellite weapons. While early use by both countries might be advantageous in a conventional war, the benefits could be short-lived. Moscow and Beijing would both have to weigh whether it was more important to slow the Americans down or avoid a war in space that could wipe out their own fleets of satellites.

Is there enough of a threat here to justify an entirely new arm of the Pentagon? The answer is "probably not yet." As important as our military satellites are, the threat to them is relatively thin at this point. Supporters of the Space Force have really not answered the question of how a new branch of the military bureaucracy would do a better job than the current military bureaucracy, and the current U.S. leadership lacks credibility. As more of America's economy becomes space-oriented a Space Force is an inevitability. But now, in 2019? It doesn't seem to make sense.

Print Citations

CMS: Mizokami, Kyle. "Trump's Space Force Isn't the Only Military Space Program: Here's What China and Russia Are Up To." In *The Reference Shelf: New Frontiers in Space,* edited by Micah L. Issitt, 69-72. Amenia, NY: Grey House Publishing, 2019.

MLA: Mizokami, Kyle. "Trump's Space Force Isn't the Only Military Space Program: Here's What China and Russia Are Up To." *The Reference Shelf: New Frontiers in Space,* edited by Micah L. Issitt, Grey Housing Publishing, 2019, pp. 69-72.

APA: Mizokami, K. (2019). Trump's space force isn't the only military space program: Here's what China and Russia are up to. In Micah L. Issitt (Ed.), *The reference shelf: New frontiers in space* (pp. 69-72). Amenia, NY: Grey Housing Publishing.

3
Legacy of the Space Race

By NASA, via Wikimedia.

Apollo 11 astronaut Buzz Aldrin on the moon, as photographed by mission commander Neil Armstrong.

Past and Future Missions

The Apollo Program, which began in 1963 and marked one of the most important eras of American scientific development, was the first step toward what has been called the final frontier of human exploration: the journey into space. Apollo brought together scientists and engineers from around the world and saw a confluence of military competition, technological innovation, and social activism unlike anything in American history before or since. The effort to reach and study the Moon was groundbreaking in both the way it brought society together and in terms of the technological breakthroughs that made the dream of Apollo a reality. The Apollo missions deeply impacted American culture, and the reverberations of this pioneering program continue into the twenty-first century. New technologies, new ideas about space and humanity's role in the cosmos, and the ongoing globalization of culture are all linked to this seminal adventure.

A Groundbreaking Endeavor

Fictional visions fueled the earliest scientific efforts to explore space, but it was military industrial development that made these visions a reality. The key military discovery that started the development of modern space technology was the V-2 ballistic missile developed by Germany and used to bomb London during World War II. When the war ended, engineers in both Russia and the United States realized that the propulsion system used for the V-2 could potentially shoot a rocket into space. It wasn't long before enterprising engineers on both sides reasoned that this technology might be used to lift other objects into space as well.

Russia beat the United States in launching the first space satellite, *Sputnik*, into space in October of 1957. Cold War tensions were rising in the United States, and there was increasing panic that Russia would dominate space and thus the United States militarily, potentially leading to the spread of Russian-centric communism and the decline of U.S.-style capitalism. Political pressure led to U.S. engineers struggling to catch up with Russian space technology, leading to a period of intense competition called the Space Race.[1]

Russia was also first to send a living organism into space, when they included a dog named Laika on *Sputnik II* in November of 1957. The announcement of the unprecedented flight intensified fear that Russia was closing in on being able to launch heavier objects into space, perhaps even a nuclear warhead.[2] U. S. politicians allocated additional funding as engineers and scientists worked to catch up. The United States launched their first satellite, *Explorer 1*, into space in January of 1958. With this accomplishment, the new goal of the Space Race was to safely launch a human into space. Russia again achieved this goal first, launching cosmonaut Yuri Gagarin into space on April 12, 1961. Shortly thereafter, NASA sent astronaut Alan Shepard to space on the *Freedom* 7 spacecraft on May 5, 1961.[3]

After America had nearly matched Russian space travel technology, America set a new goal, one that the American public could embrace and would put the United States ahead of Russia. On May 25, 1961, President John F. Kennedy gave a speech supporting NASA's efforts and promoting the idea that humans should land on the Moon. In his famous speech at Rice University, Kennedy encouraged all Americans to embrace, as a national goal, the effort to land an American astronaut on the Moon by the end of the decade. The goal was framed as among the greatest challenges in the history of mankind, as America's chance to grasp international technological superiority, and as a patriotic expression of American ingenuity and work ethic. As Kennedy famously described the challenge: "We choose to go to the moon. We choose to go to the moon in this decade and do the other things, not because they are easy, but because they are hard, because that goal will serve to organize and measure the best of our energies and skills, because that challenge is one that we are willing to accept, one we are unwilling to postpone, and one which we intend to win."[4]

Successes and Tragedy

Kennedy's speech galvanized Americans, and the Apollo Program was organized. The initial missions, known as SA-1 through SA-5, were unmanned missions intended to test the capabilities of America's new rocket, the *Saturn 1* launch vehicle. Missions A-101 through A-105 tested Saturn 1's ability to launch equipment similar to the Apollo spacecraft that would eventually be launched into space. This was followed by four missions to test the abort and emergency systems on board the spacecraft, then three missions utilizing an updated rocket design, the *Saturn 1B*, while carrying a mockup of the Apollo spacecraft.

Initially, the flight known as *Apollo 1* was named AS-204, during which three astronauts—Roger B. Chaffee, Virgil "Gus" Grissom, and Edward H. White—tested launch pad procedures. During the test on January 27, 1967, a fire broke out aboard the spacecraft, killing all three astronauts. The mission was renamed *Apollo 1* in their honor. The *Apollo 1* disaster shocked the nation, providing a visceral demonstration of the dangers involved in the program. An investigation and Congressional hearings followed to determine if there had been any negligence, and it was unclear if the program would resume. Ultimately, politicians allowed the program to continue, and NASA found ways to enhance safety aboard subsequent versions of Apollo spacecraft.[5]

NASA did not designate Apollo missions 2 and 3, and resumed testing with missions 4 through 6—unmanned missions designed to test their newest iteration of the Saturn rocket, the *Saturn V*. The historic *Apollo 7* (AS-205) was the first manned mission into space. Astronauts Walter M. Schirra, Donn F. Eisele, and Walter Cunningham reached space on October 11, 1968, and spent more time in space orbiting the earth than all previous Soviet missions combined. Apollo 7 provided Americans with an initial show of perceived superiority in the Space Race.

Several months later, NASA sent James A. Lovell, Frank Borman, and William A. Anders to the Moon in *Apollo 8*, with the three astronauts becoming the first to orbit an extraterrestrial body. *Apollo 8* was truly groundbreaking and some historians believe that it had more transformative impact on ideas about space and science than the Apollo missions that followed.

Walking on the Moon

Following *Apollo 8*, two additional missions tested the technology that would be used to land on the lunar surface. *Apollo 9* tested the lunar module (LM) in space, and *Apollo 10* tested the systems and procedures that would be used for the moon landing, without actually landing on the moon. This honor would go to *Apollo 11* and astronauts Neil Armstrong, Buzz Aldrin, and Michael Collins. On July 16, 1969, *Apollo 11* achieved the goal that Kennedy set for the nation, to land on the moon before the end of the decade. Armstrong became the first man to walk on the moon's surface, and famously said at that moment, "One small step for a man, one giant leap for mankind," words that have become a famous part of Apollo's legacy on Earth. Armstrong's words are often misquoted as "One small step for man," rather than "One small step for **a** man."

There were six additional Apollo Missions. *Apollo 12* saw a second successful moon landing and collected important samples of Moon rock. The next mission, *Apollo 13*, is remembered for the famous phrase, "Houston, we've had a problem," spoken by astronaut James Lovell when the *Apollo 13* craft suffered a serious and potentially deadly problem—the lunar landing was aborted after an oxygen tank in the service module exploded two days into the mission. Speaking of the incident, Lovell recalled, "Our mission was a failure but I like to think it was a successful failure," referring to the safe return of the astronauts. Outside of the resounding success of *Apollo 11*, the *Apollo 13* mission and the dedicated experts who cooperated to save the crew is perhaps the best-known story of the Apollo saga.[6]

Legacy of the Apollo Program

At the height of Apollo, scientists and engineers working on the nation's space program hoped that continued effort and innovation would result in sending humans far beyond the sphere of Earth and its satellite, perhaps reaching Mars, but this would not come to pass. The Apollo Program continued through *Apollo 17*, with subsequent missions revealing new information about the lunar surface, bringing back color photography of the moon and Earth from the lunar surface, but enthusiasm for the project waned. The decline of the space program, and the abandonment of the Apollo Program, has been justified in part by the tremendous cost, in part by fluctuations in global and domestic climate, and in part by global developments that eliminated Russian competition.

The legacy of the Apollo Program is wide-reaching. Many consumer products and familiar technological innovations began with innovations developed during the Space Race. Freeze-dried meals, the Dustbuster, and memory foam mattresses all began as products for space missions. The Apollo missions inspired a generation of scientists, engineers, and pilots, and generally transformed the popular conception of space. One of the most enduring signifiers of the Apollo Program's cultural importance can be seen in the conspiracy theories claiming that one or more of the Moon landings were faked. This idea has become a pop-culture trope, appearing in many works of fiction. Disbelief is in fact a natural reaction to such a feat, a feat that redefined humanity's relationship to their planet and their universe, dispelling millennia-old myths about the cosmos.

Works Used

George, Alice. "The Sad, Sad Story of Laika, the Space Dog, and Her One-Way Trip into Orbit." *Smithsonian*. Apr 11, 2018.

"John F. Kennedy Moon Speech—Rice Stadium." *NASA*. Retrieved from https://er.jsc.nasa.gov/seh/ricetalk.htm.

Kernan, Michael. "The Space Race." *Smithsonian*. Aug 1997. Retrieved from https://www.smithsonianmag.com/history/the-space-race-141404095/.

Larimer, Sarah. "'We Have a Fire in the Cockpit!' The Apollo 1 Disaster 50 Years Later." *The Washington Post*. Jan 26, 2017. Retrieved from https://www.washingtonpost.com/news/speaking-of-science/wp/2017/01/26/50-years-ago-three-astronauts-died-in-the-apollo-1-fire/.

Lovell, Jim. "Houston, We've Had a Problem," Apollo Expeditions to the Moon. NASA. Retrieved from https://history.nasa.gov/SP-350/ch-13-1.html.

Redd, Nola Taylor. "Alan Shepard: First American in Space." *Space*. Oct 10, 2018.

Notes

1. Kernan, "The Space Race."
2. George, "The Sad, Sad Story of Laika, the Space Dog, and Her One-Way Trip into Orbit."
3. Redd, "Alan Shepard: First American in Space."
4. "John F. Kennedy Moon Speech—Rice Stadium," *NASA*.
5. Larimer, "'We Have a Fire in the Cockpit!' The Apollo 1 Disaster 50 Years Later."
6. Lovell, "Houston, We've Had a Problem."

Apollo Was NASA's Biggest Win—But Its Legacy Is Holding the Agency Back

By Loren Grush

The Verge, July 16, 2019

"There are few things in life that we could look back on and say that have regressed since 1969," Mark Sirangelo, who recently helped to lead NASA's Moon return plans before departing in May, tells *The Verge*. "And I could say, very objectively, that human spaceflight in America has gone backwards."

The agency's latest human spaceflight flagship is the Artemis mission. Its goal is to establish a long-term presence near the Moon and put the first woman on the lunar surface. To get Artemis off the ground, NASA is using much of the same established infrastructure it's used since the dawn of the space age. Just like it did 50 years ago, the agency is insisting on building and overseeing the most crucial pieces of hardware itself: the rockets and spacecraft. But this Apollo-era model requires massive space budgets that haven't materialized since the Cold War, leading to delays and stagnation as workers attempt to do more complicated work with less resources. Compounding the problem, a national sense of urgency is simply missing. Instead, NASA is at the whims of lawmakers who prioritize employment in their districts over finding the most efficient route to deep space.

Many of these things must change before the United States can once again take up a position at the vanguard of human exploration. A return to Apollo's glory days will require a different hardware pipeline, a new funding structure, and a soul-searching assessment of NASA's role in the entire process. And there needs to be more clarity about why NASA is doing any of this at all.

"I think it's a mess to assume that NASA has to be all about humans going into deep space to be important and of value," Lori Garver, the former deputy administrator of NASA under the Obama administration, tells *The Verge*. "And I think that is the mess of Apollo."

The Apollo Precedent

Apollo's success is inextricable from its context. The missions took place at the height of the Cold War, when the United States was looking for ways to show off its strength against the Soviet Union. Advisors to President John F. Kennedy told him that the best way to beat the Soviets in space was to send a man to the Moon. So in

1962, Kennedy publicly promised to send humans to the lunar surface by the end of the decade in his famous speech at Rice University.

Driven by patriotic one-upmanship, Congress followed through and supported the initiative. NASA's budget increased, swelling from $500 million a year in 1960 to more than $5 billion in 1965, according to NASA. At the time, that was about 4.31 percent of the overall federal budget. Today, NASA only receives about 0.5 percent of the annual federal budget.

Still, support was tenuous at best. Throughout the 1960s, up to 60 percent of the US population opposed how much money the government was spending on the Apollo initiative. At one point, Congress was poised to reduce the amount of money for the program, and Kennedy himself became concerned that the pros of Apollo didn't outweigh the cons.

Then in 1963, Kennedy was assassinated. In the aftermath, the new president, Lyndon B. Johnson determined that Kennedy's ambitious dream should become reality. Johnson called for an increase in funds to NASA's budget and maintained funding for the Apollo program through the pivotal Apollo 11 mission. "No Congress, no subsequent president could dare to take that away from the memory of Kennedy," Robert Pearlman, a space historian and founder of collectSPACE, tells *The Verge*. "Even Nixon understood completely—he couldn't cancel Apollo until after it was achieved or the Russians won."

But once Apollo succeeded, its necessity in the eyes of politicians quickly diminished, and crewed landings came to an end in 1972. Eventually, the Cold War ended, too, leaving the United States without a human spaceflight rival to measure themselves against. "The perfect storm that set up Apollo will never exist again," says Pearlman.

What Apollo Left Behind

Fifty years later, Apollo's ghost still haunts our space agency. The program created an expectation that NASA must always have some kind of flagship human exploration initiative. "That notion of having a big central government program that was going to manage this frontier—to manage this whole zone of activity for human exploration and eventually for robots—was really born," Jim Muncy, founder of PoliSpace, a space policy consulting agency, tells *The Verge*.

Over the last few decades, presidents including both Bushes, Obama, and now Trump, have all proposed big human spaceflight endeavors like sending people to the Moon and Mars. Each of these lofty plans have floundered, and one of the biggest reasons is money; NASA just hasn't received the same substantial budget boost it received during Apollo. "Now what we have is the structure of [Apollo], except we don't have a national crisis," says Muncy. "There's plenty of other things for people to work on, and they can't hire as many people as they did back then, because they don't have as much money." Instead of a devoted human spaceflight budget, if NASA needs extra funding, administrations are often forced to cut within the space agency itself. The result is that other areas of NASA—like planetary science,

Earth science, astrophysics, education, and more—get cannibalized to meet the "worthier" goal.

Whatever money NASA can scrape together is poured into an established system that dates to the earliest days of the space program. Apollo created an army of contractors and built NASA centers with expertise in building rockets. Now— long after the program's end—both remain hungry for contracts and jobs from the space agency. NASA has obliged, and continues to use these institutions to spearhead the agency's big-

> **Numerous government audits and investigations have found problems with NASA's sprawling way of managing human exploration.**

gest projects and build rocket hardware. "For a large contractor, you know your job is stable," Laura Forczyk, a space consultant and owner of space research and consulting firm Astralytical, tells *The Verge*. "That's the way NASA operates, with these really large contracts that extend on and on, year after year."

A prime example is Boeing. The company, along with North American Aviation and Douglas Aircraft Company, were the biggest contractors on the Saturn V rocket that took humans to the Moon during the Apollo era. Now Boeing, which acquired Douglas and North American, is the prime contractor on the Space Launch System—the giant rocket NASA is building to take humans into deep space. It was also one of the biggest contractors for the Space Shuttle and the US component of the International Space Station. Other companies like Lockheed Martin, Northrop Grumman, and Aerojet Rocketdyne all have ties to Apollo and continue to work on NASA's biggest projects today.

"What Apollo did was create a space industrial complex," John Logsdon, founder of the Space Policy Institute at George Washington University, tells *The Verge*.

NASA centers like Marshall Space Flight Center in Alabama, Stennis Space Center in Mississippi, and Michoud Assembly Facility in Louisiana were built for the Apollo program, and continue to build rocket hardware for the agency. They create thousands of jobs and are putting billions of dollars into local economies.

"Across the exploration portfolio—the Orion spacecraft, the Space Launch System rocket, the exploration grounds systems that comprise the ability to fly the rocket and the spacecraft and launch it—we've got all 50 states involved. And it's a lot of jobs across the United States," Mike Sarafin, the Artemis mission manager at NASA, tells *The Verge*. All of these companies, centers, and states have become accustomed to getting these jobs and contracts, without much competition or urgency to deliver.

"We have been building to the infrastructure and centers versus building a program that is responsive to the needs of the country in current times," says Garver. "Because we had those centers, and we had to use them. And same with the people. It's almost impossible to imagine what you would do differently without that, but you wouldn't recreate them."

Changing the Status Quo

Numerous government audits and investigations have found problems with NASA's sprawling way of managing human exploration. These organizational problems are perhaps one of the biggest reasons NASA hasn't reached any major human space-flight milestones on par with Apollo, according to Sirangelo. "People look at the technology as the only piece of the puzzle," he says. "But oftentimes, it's the way you manage the technology. It's the way that you manage the contracting. It's how you set up the program. Those things need to be innovative as well."

After all this time, getting rid of the army left by Apollo is tricky. The SLS program alone supports more than 25,000 jobs across the country and is responsible for an economic output of $4.75 billion, according to NASA's Marshall Space Flight Center. Uprooting people's livelihoods can be devastating. And because NASA human exploration missions have sustained a lot of jobs in the South, many southern lawmakers are hellbent on keeping this employment intact.

Just look what happened when the Obama administration tried to cancel Bush's Constellation program, an effort to send people back to the Moon. The White House claimed the budget needed to sustain Constellation just wasn't realistic. But cancellation didn't sit well with lawmakers whose constituents were about to lose a bunch of jobs, according to Garver.

"Some of the people within NASA who were really committed to keeping these jobs sold Congress, and we were given an ultimatum that we had to do a big rocket, or we wouldn't get commercial crew, and the technology programs, and the Earth sciences programs that we wanted," says Garver. "So we took the deal."

The Constellation rocket morphed into the Space Launch System, and NASA has been working on it ever since. And lawmakers like Richard Shelby (R-AL) or Mo Brooks (R-AL), who represent the districts where the rocket is being built in Alabama, will defend it at all costs. Meanwhile, the SLS has cost NASA around $14 billion so far over the last decade. It was originally supposed to fly in 2017, but probably won't fly until 2021.

This mentality preserves economies, but makes it difficult to achieve NASA's long-term goals—something Blue Origin founder Jeff Bezos has pointed out. "Now your objective is not to get a man to the Moon, or a woman to the Moon, but to get a woman to the Moon while preserving X number of jobs in my district," Bezos said during a talk, according to *GeekWire*. "That is a complexifier, and not a healthy one… They didn't have that back in 1961 and 1962. They were moving fast."

The Commercial Option

The agency will have to change how it does business, or it will remain stuck in the same repetitive cycle. Fortunately, a burgeoning private space industry may provide NASA with a way out of the loop.

For the longest time, NASA *was* the leader in creating rockets that could get a lot of stuff into space at once. There simply weren't any options for outsourcing this kind of development to companies outside the space industrial complex. That's starting to change. Companies like SpaceX, Blue Origin, and the United Launch

Alliance (an outgrowth of Lockheed Martin and Boeing) are developing less expensive rockets.

"What if the answer for putting humans to the Moon was: we let Blue Origin and SpaceX and other companies compete against each other for how to do that?" says Muncy. "And we'll buy from the ones that we think have the smartest approach, and we'll partner with them."

In some ways, that's exactly what NASA is trying to do. The agency selected various companies to send robotic landers to the Moon, and NASA officials claim commercial rockets will be needed in the lunar return. Additionally, NASA plans to select one or two companies to build human lunar landers in their own way, without as much agency oversight. "It's an 'and' approach where we're using the stalwarts of the aerospace industry and some new entrants," says Sarafin.

The problem is that the private industry hasn't fully surpassed NASA yet. Some vehicles like SpaceX's Falcon Heavy and ULA's Delta IV Heavy are reliably flying, but many of the more ambitious projects promised by commercial companies have yet to take shape. NASA's Commercial Crew Program—an experiment to see if the commercial space industry can take the reins of sending people to low Earth orbit—was first funded in 2010, but has yet to actually fly any astronauts due to struggles in development.

While commercial space is finding its footing, NASA is inextricable from almost any major American space endeavor. Its guidance is needed to jump-start big initiatives—especially since there is no obvious market yet for sending people into deep space. And private industry really needs NASA's money. The agency's investment can often make or break a space startup, even for the largest players on the stage today. SpaceX, one of NASA's biggest partners, owes its success in large part to NASA development contracts it received as it was getting off the ground.

Until the commercial space industry starts to repeatedly fly giant rockets more often than NASA does, the agency will probably continue to build its own vehicles. "There are just a lot of promises, and we can see the history of how much companies have overpromised and under-delivered," says Forczyk. "It is really a bit of a Catch-22 in that you want to open up the possibilities for including commercial players, but there's multiple companies who have not yet proven themselves. But Can They Prove Themselves Without The Massive Funding?"

But Why?

Breaking down the Apollo model has been NASA's biggest challenge for decades, and perhaps one of the key ways that NASA can overcome this is by articulating *why* we need to send humans into deep space so badly. The current White House claims the goal is to maintain American leadership in space, harvest materials on the Moon and help the commercial sector. Those goals aren't measuring up to the passion ignited by the Red Scare and the national mourning of a slain president.

The current administration is trying to push NASA to accelerate their timelines to create a feeling of urgency once again. In March, Vice President Mike Pence challenged the agency to put humans on the lunar surface in 2024 instead of 2028 as originally planned. But even with a time crunch, NASA is struggling to get a requested $1.6 billion boost in funds from Congress. The House ignored this increase when drafting a budget for NASA for 2020, and lawmakers have expressed concern over the cost of a lunar initiative and where the money will be coming from.

Compared to the piles of money bulldozed over to NASA by Congress in the 1960s, the trickle of funds is damning. Domestically, there's no need for politicians outside the districts that house NASA contractors and centers to push for increased funds. And from a foreign policy perspective, no other superpower poses enough of a threat to spur a substantial space race once again. Many experts looked to China as a potential motivator, as the country expanded its efforts in space by launching robotic landers to the Moon and by sending humans to a space station in low Earth orbit. But some argue China's ambitions are not lofty enough to spur action from the United States. "The Chinese landing on the Moon with rovers that we did 40 years ago, it's not the same," says Garver. "It's not threatening."

Ultimately, it's going to be difficult to sustain anything ambitious when the public support for deep-space human exploration is even lower now than it was under Apollo. So until NASA can articulate the need of doing another Moon program or going to Mars, any growth will move slowly—as long as the Apollo paradigm lives on. "You don't have to create a war, we have to create a purpose," says Sirangelo.

Apollo had a purpose. It was a major relay in the Space Race, and it showcased the incredible feats of engineering people can achieve when they bend their wills toward a common, monumental goal. It let people dream, and inspired innovation. But if NASA can't find a new purpose that motivates in the same way as the Cold War did, it's possible that the agency may remain trapped in its current cycle of development for human exploration for some time. The agency *is* trying to break out of this mold, but the politics of NASA and the space industrial complex that have been developing rocket hardware for decades make it difficult to evolve. And the agency may have the Apollo program to thank.

Print Citations

CMS: Grush, Loren. "Apollo Was NASA's Biggest Win—But Its Legacy Is Holding the Agency Back." In *The Reference Shelf: New Frontiers in Space,* edited by Micah L. Issitt, 79-84. Amenia, NY: Grey House Publishing, 2019.

MLA: Grush, Loren. "Apollo Was NASA's Biggest Win—But Its Legacy Is Holding the Agency Back." *The Reference Shelf: New Frontiers in Space,* edited by Micah L. Issitt, Grey Housing Publishing, 2019, pp. 79-84.

APA: Grush, L. (2019). Apollo was NASA's biggest win—But its legacy is holding the agency back. In Micah L. Issitt (Ed.), *The reference shelf: New frontiers in space* (pp. 79-84). Amenia, NY: Grey Housing Publishing.

Many People Still Believe the Moon Landing Was Fake: But Who's Profiting?

By Rebecca Jennings
Vox, June 24, 2019

The first step on the path to recovery is admitting that the more you listen to moon landing conspiracy theories, the more you start to believe them.

What finally got me were the crosshairs. Crosshairs! The word itself sounds like it belongs on a bulletin board covered with a laserlike web of red yarn. But you tell me why some of the camera's crosshairs appeared to be *behind* objects in NASA's moon landing photos? You can't!

It turns out, though, you can. You can also disprove literally every moon landing conspiracy claim, of which there are many dozens. On July 20, 1969, the Apollo 11 Lunar Module landed on the moon. We have irrefutable proof of this; still, anywhere from 6 to 20 percent of Americans do not believe it actually happened, depending on your source, with an additional (and far more bewildering) 5 percent who said in a 1999 Gallup poll that they were "undecided."

But the moon landing hoax theory has persisted for decades due to the simple fact that if you don't think about it too hard, it sort of makes sense. The motive is there: The US really wanted to beat the Soviet Union to the moon, and Sputnik forced NASA into action. The technology was there (although this *Adam Ruins Everything* segment explains why actually, it wasn't), because *2001: A Space Odyssey* had come out a year before and showed realistic footage of a studio-simulated space.

Plus, the feat seemed physically impossible: Wouldn't the Van Allen radiation belts kill astronauts before they got to the moon? (No, because the spaceship only moved through them for a few hours, not days.) And how were computers from the '60s supposed to launch a rocket that went 239,000 miles? Weren't they basically just calculators? Seems fake!

And then there is the dubious physical evidence of the moon landing, which has been dissected by conspiracy theorists for decades. In photos, shadows appear at multiple angles, but shouldn't there just be a single light source in space, the sun? Why was the American flag waving when there is no wind in a vacuum? Why wasn't there a crater where the Apollo landed? Why would astronauts' boots make footprints when there's no water on the moon? What about the crosshairs? The crosshairs!!!

This is only a sampling of supposed evidence that the moon landing was faked, all of which has been debunked, repeatedly, for decades. And yet a steady gurgling of moon truther ephemera has remained since the 1970s, from books to documentaries and now, YouTube videos. Someone must benefit from insisting that Neil Armstrong and Buzz Aldrin didn't walk on the moon, right? Otherwise, why would so many people still believe it?

So I did what conspiracy theorists do, and followed the money.

Moon Landing Conspiracy Theories Began with a Self-Published Book

To understand who's making money off moon landing conspiracy theories, you have to go back in history, starting with the first major book written about it. What would you call your book about the fact that we never went to the moon?

We Never Went to the Moon (subhead: "America's Thirty Billion Dollar Swindle") was written in 1976 by a man called Bill Kaysing, who according to the tribute website BillKaysing.com was also known as "Wild Bill Kaysing" and is widely considered the father of moon landing hoax theories. (Kaysing died in 2005.)

Kaysing's claim to expertise was that in the early 1960s, he had worked as a technical writer for Rocketdyne, a rocket design and production company, and alleged that the job had given him access to documents proving that the Apollo mission was a hoax.

But because Kaysing self-published his seminal book, it's impossible to know how much money he actually made from inventing one of the most popular conspiracy theories of all time. He spent the rest of his life appearing on talk shows, likely for modest sums of money, and went on to write and self-publish other books called *How to Eat Well for a Dollar a Day*. Kaysing was also critical of corporations and "Madison Avenue" and advocated for the homeless, according to his website.

Paperback editions of *We Never Went to the Moon* are currently being sold on Amazon for the rather high price of $44.99, though it is also the 921,946th most popular book on the website, which is not very popular. Someone is making money, however, but it is not Kaysing; instead, it is the CreateSpace Independent Publishing Platform, which is owned by Amazon.

$$$: Probably very little, but at least some of it is going to Amazon!

One Television Network Definitely Made Money off the Moon Landing Conspiracy

One of the programs Kaysing appeared on was a controversial 2001 Fox TV special called "Conspiracy Theory: Did We Land on the Moon?" which effectively answers its titular question with a big "no." It presented evidence that suggested that NASA had faked the moon landing, and sparked considerable doubt among the public. In 2002, one of the conspiracy theorists who appeared on the Fox show harassed Buzz Aldrin on the street, asking him to swear on the Bible that he actually went to the moon. Aldrin then punched him in the face, and there is a video of it.

Fox officials claimed to the Salt Lake City paper *Deseret News* that after "Did We

Land on the Moon?" aired, American skepticism of the moon landing increased to 20 percent, and afterward, the *Today* show aired a debate about it. But did Fox make money off it?

The same article states that the 47-minute program aired to about 15 million people, which would have translated to about 13 minutes of commercials in an hour-long slot. Today, the only shows that garner 15 million viewers are the really big ones—we'll use as an example CBS's hit show *NCIS*, which had more than 15 million viewers over the 2018-'19 season. A 30-second ad spot for NCIS in 2018 cost about $136,000, according to Ad Age. In 2001 dollars, that's $96,074.10—multiply that by 26, for a total of 13 minutes of advertising, and that's $2,597,926.60 worth of ad dollars. This is, obviously, an extremely imperfect science but a helpful ballpark!

$$$: At least a couple million for Fox and ultimately for Rupert Murdoch, who wouldn't consider that very much money at all.

But Are Any Moon Truthers Making Money on YouTube?

Even though many of the original moon truthers who appeared on TV talk shows and documentaries throughout the '90s and early 2000s are now dead, there has to be a new generation of hucksters on the most conspiracy theory-friendly platform of the 21st century, right?

Wrong, although this may be more of a recent development. Now that there have been several violent crimes committed by people radicalized via YouTube videos, the company has said that it will recommend fewer conspiracy theory videos, and those expressing doubt about widely accepted events will include an informational text box linking to third-party sources.

> As in most economies, the moon landing conspiracy economy drives the money all the way to the top: the top booksellers, TV networks, and the top YouTubers.

Plus, making money strictly off YouTube advertisements is increasingly difficult, and most moon landing conspiracy videos are virtually harmless considering their low production value or lack of substantial views, like my favorite example of a guy in sunglasses and a yellow vest combing through the original moon landing issue of *National Geographic*. (Hilariously, the pre-roll advertisement I got for this video was a MasterClass with NASA astronaut Chris Hadfield.)

There is one exception to this: Shane Dawson, who built a subscriber base of 22 million in part by making conspiracy theory videos aimed at teens and kids. His moon landing video, which has 7 million views, stops short of saying that he actually believes NASA faked the moon landing, but admits it was what sparked his interest in conspiracy theories.

After presenting all the evidence, he says, "It's not a shock, because the government fakes so much shit. I mean, we've talked about 9/11, we've talked about crisis actors. Why wouldn't the moon landing be fake? Why wouldn't we fake that, just to win over other countries? It makes you wonder, have we actually ever been to the moon?"

This video is making money for Dawson—there are ads on it, and there is notably not one of YouTube's Apollo 11 disclaimer boxes in the description. According to Social Blade, which tracks YouTubers' stats and estimated earnings, a video with 7 million views would earn him anywhere between $3,500 and $28,000, depending on ad revenue.

$$$: Somewhere between $3,500 and $28,000.

Seems Like the Money Keeps Rising to the Top! Hmm!

The average YouTuber isn't Shane Dawson, however, and neither is the average moon landing truther. Dawson seems to be one of the few individuals making actual money off peddling moon landing conspiracy theories. But notably, his moon landing video isn't anywhere near his most-viewed conspiracy videos, so one couldn't argue that Dawson is making his living off the moon landing theory alone.

As in most economies, the moon landing conspiracy economy drives the money all the way to the top: The top booksellers (Amazon), the top TV networks (Fox), and the top YouTubers (Dawson). Which means that those who benefit the most from people believing in moon landing conspiracies are those already in power! Maybe that's why some of our most visible truthers are very famous celebrities: Kyrie Irving, Steph Curry (though he later said he was joking), Frank Ocean, Whoopi Goldberg, Marion Cotillard.

Meanwhile, true believers like Bill Kaysing and his modern-day counterparts like Martin Kenny and *Did We Go?* director Aron Ranen are left to appear for presumably little money on documentaries and TV spots in which they make Glenn Beck sound like the rational one. They are, one could argue, but lowly foot soldiers in the establishment's war to brainwash Americans into believing we didn't actually go to the moon.

I Am the Conspiracy Theorist Now

This is obviously a conspiracy theory itself, but it is one that, much like the moon landing hoax, I am starting to believe the more I think about it. Maybe the question is no longer "Did we go to the moon?" but "Who benefits by suggesting that we didn't?" Am I the conspiracy theorist, or is perpetuating conspiracy theories as entertainment a far greater danger to society?

Let us begin again with the facts: On July 20, 1969, the Apollo 11 Lunar Module landed on the moon. Today, 50 years later, we live in a world in which people have threatened to kill others, spurred by their belief in conspiracy theories, in a country whose president has propagated more than a dozen of them as though they were fact.

Conspiracy theories have become so normalized in the latter half of the 2010s that the most publicized ones involve things like a secret network of omnipotent celebrities, a child sex ring run by Democratic politicians, or the earth being literally flat. These are wild things to genuinely, actually believe, yet they come at the same time that a "fact" has come to mean whatever audiences feel like believing.

I personally do not think the moon landing hoax theory will suddenly become extremely popular in our current cultural moment, however, and here is why: The moon landing has nothing to do with you or me. It does not directly implicate the self, which is all human beings' favorite subject. Claims that vaccines cause autism or that a single vegetable is covertly wreaking havoc on the guts of all Americans or that putting a $66 egg up one's vagina will "regulate your hormones" are all bullshit, of course. But believing them allows us to expend further mental energy on ourselves, which we very much love to do.

These beliefs then also get to become part of our identities: You become someone who "can't eat corn" or someone who makes a "brave" choice for their children, even if that choice puts people in danger.

In comparison to all these things, the belief that the moon landing was shot in a Hollywood studio actually seems sort of quaint. How cute, a theory that probably won't end up hurting someone! Perhaps on the 50th anniversary of the NASA moon landing—which definitely happened—we can appreciate the moon landing conspiracy for what it was: a mostly harmless piece of entertainment that possibly also led to the normalization of conspiracies in general, which *is* harmful.

Anyway, on July 20, 1969, the Apollo 11 Lunar Module landed on the moon. The end!

Print Citations

CMS: Jennings, Rebecca. "Many People Still Believe the Moon Landing Was Fake: But Who's Profiting?" In *The Reference Shelf: New Frontiers in Space,* edited by Micah L. Issitt, 85-89. Amenia, NY: Grey House Publishing, 2019.

MLA: Jennings, Rebecca. "Many People Still Believe the Moon Landing Was Fake: But Who's Profiting?" *The Reference Shelf: New Frontiers in Space,* edited by Micah L. Issitt, Grey Housing Publishing, 2019, pp. 85-89.

APA: Jennings, R. (2019). Many people still believe the Moon landing was fake: But who's profiting? In Micah L. Issitt (Ed.), *The reference shelf: New frontiers in space* (pp. 85-89). Amenia, NY: Grey Housing Publishing.

Q&A: Shuttle Astronaut Mike Massimino on the Legacy of Apollo 11

By Jennifer Leman
Scientific American, July 19, 2019

Fifty years ago a six-year-old boy named Michael Massimino sat in front of his family's television on Long Island, N.Y., transfixed by the blurry black-and-white images of a man walking on the moon. Like millions of other children watching the *Apollo 11* lunar landing on July 20, 1969, Massimino vowed to one day become an astronaut just like the *Apollo 11* crewmembers he so revered—Neil Armstrong, Buzz Aldrin and Michael Collins. Most of his starry-eyed generation would remain earthbound, trapped and discouraged by the transience of the Apollo era, which fizzled out with the last human landing in 1972. But Massimino managed to persevere, pursuing his Apollo-inspired dream through decades of deliberate preparation and multiple setbacks, ultimately joining NASA's astronaut corps in 1996.

The formative influence of the Apollo missions is a common thread woven through the personal stories of nearly all the men and women who have subsequently voyaged to space. Not all, however, were as fortunate as Massimino, who managed to befriend many of the Apollo astronauts during his NASA career. When he finally lifted off, riding space shuttles skyward in 2002 and in 2009 to service the Hubble Space Telescope, he carried their lessons with him. Returning to Earth, he built on their inspirational legacy, using his own spaceflight experience to become a celebrated popularizer of space science and exploration. After his retirement from NASA in 2014, motivating the next generation of astronauts remained one of Massimino's passions; today he is a professor at Columbia University and senior advisor at the Intrepid Sea, Air & Space Museum in Manhattan.

On the eve of the 50th anniversary of the first lunar landing, *Scientific American* spoke with Massimino about the impact that the Apollo missions have had on his own career trajectory and on the world.

You were six years old when *Apollo 11* launched and landed on the moon. What do you remember from the mission?

Apollo 11 was one of the first news events that I remember occurring, when I became aware of things. I remember the buildup to the mission that summer, and I remember watching the launch from my summer recreation program at my

elementary school in Long
Island. I remember watch-
ing [the landing] in the living room. I was there with
my family, and I was just
riveted to the television set.

> **It wasn't just an American accomplishment. It was truly a human accomplishment for the whole world.**

I remember them landing and everyone being very, very happy that they made it. I went outside and looked up at the moon thinking, "There are people on it." I wanted to be one of those guys. All three of the *Apollo 11* astronauts were the coolest guys ever. Neil Armstrong was my hero, and I liked Mike Collins because he had the same name as I did. At six years old, that's very important. I was very excited about it. I think it just hit me at the right time in my life.

I knew it was a great accomplishment for everybody, but I knew it also meant something more to me. We were learning about Columbus and other explorers when I was in school, stuff that happened 500 years earlier. And I thought to myself, this is what they're going to learn about in school 500 years from now. They're going to learn about *this*. This is when we left the planet.

You went on to become an astronaut and, over time, became familiar with the entire *Apollo 11* crew. Tell me about those interactions. Did they give you any valuable advice?

The first thing I asked Neil Armstrong was, when did he think of his saying: "one small step for man, one giant leap for mankind." He said he didn't think about it until after he landed. I was a new astronaut, and he said, "if I didn't land it, there'd be no reason to say anything." I think he saw it as a teachable moment. He told me, "Mike, you're new at this. You gotta stick to business first and worry about all that later." That was what I learned from Neil Armstrong.

The first time I met Buzz Aldrin, I introduced myself, but he was busy and I didn't have much of a conversation with him. I did get to interview him at the Intrepid Museum five years ago, on the 45th anniversary of *Apollo 11*. We talked about what he famously called the moon's "magnificent desolation," his realization when he got out of the lunar lander and looked around that everything there had not really changed in hundreds of thousands, maybe millions of years. I see him from time to time at different places. He's polite enough to pretend like he remembers who I am, so that's kinda cool!

I first met Mike Collins before I was an astronaut, when I was an intern down at NASA headquarters. I heard him give a little talk, and when I went to the cafeteria for lunch, he was there sitting by himself. I forced myself on him and said, "Hey, do you mind if I join you?" He said, "sure." I told him I was a student at M.I.T., and we talked about various things going on at NASA. Since then we've reconnected. When our mutual friend, [Apollo and Skylab] astronaut Alan Bean, died a little over a year ago, I spoke at Alan's memorial and was an honorary pallbearer at his interment, and Mike was there, too. It just so happened that we got to spend some time together there. He's a very nice man. Very, very humble.

Were there any challenging moments during your own spaceflights when your discussions with them proved useful?

Yes. When I was going to do the first tweet from space, I took Neil's advice—I didn't plan it. That was probably a mistake because when the time came I didn't know what to say, and basically my tweet ended up getting made fun of on *Saturday Night Live*. So I was like, "I don't know, Neil, if that was the best advice!" I probably should have thought about what I was going to tweet a little bit more.

But certainly, as astronauts we all benefit from what those guys did. When people think of astronauts, they think of Neil and Buzz and Mike, and the original Mercury Seven and what those guys were to the country and what the space program meant back then. We're still benefiting from that; we're still following in their footsteps.

You know, some people might say that after Apollo we took a step back in space, but I think we actually started looking a little more long-term, which is what led to the space shuttles, the Hubble Space Telescope and the International Space Station—where we now have a permanent presence in space. People have been up there since 2000! So we learned how to live and work in space for long periods of time. In some ways that's nowhere near as impressive as what we did with Apollo, but that more steady program is what will lead us back to the moon. When we go back, I think it will be to stay.

Why do you think the Apollo missions, in particular, still resonate with so many people around the world?

They were the first times that humans left our planet and truly went to another place. I think that was seen globally as an accomplishment that everyone could be proud of and could be a part of. It wasn't just an American accomplishment. It was truly a human accomplishment for the whole world.

I don't think [the Apollo astronauts] realized the effect it would have on the entire world. Alan Bean, who was on *Apollo 12*, told me that when he traveled the world after his flight, it didn't matter what country he was in, the response wasn't "You Americans did it." It was, "*We* did it. The world did it."

What do you think the 50th anniversary of *Apollo 11* should mean to people today—particularly younger people who weren't around to witness it?

The 50th anniversary is an opportunity for them to learn about it. Luckily, we still have some of the Apollo astronauts left. I was at a 40th anniversary celebration at the National Air and Space Museum 10 years ago, after my second space flight, and all three of the *Apollo 11* crew were there. Neil was still alive. I think just about all the moonwalkers were there—they were in their late seventies, early eighties at the time.

Now, 10 years later, there are not so many of them around. But there's still enough of them alive to tell the story of Apollo, and hopefully this celebration goes on not just for *Apollo 11,* but for the remaining missions. And not just for the astronauts, but also people who worked in the control room, people who worked behind the scenes to make these things happen.

I still think it resonates with NASA, with our country and with the world that if you can land a man on the moon, you can do anything. You hear it all the time: "We can land a man on the moon, but how come I can't get a decent cup of coffee?" It's a reference to the miraculous things that we can accomplish. We've got to keep that in mind when we're thinking of other problems today that seem to be impossible.

The White House wants NASA to return astronauts to the lunar surface by 2024. Do you think that's a realistic deadline?

There's no doubt that we could get there by 2024, because we have rockets and spacecraft under construction that could do it. Now, the question is, what are we going to do when we get there? If we're landing there, are we going to try to stay and build a habitat? What are we going to do? I certainly think the first steps could be taken by 2024, and I don't see any reason why we couldn't do that. I think that's a good goal, actually.

If you had the opportunity to go to the moon, what would you be most interested in seeing or doing?

I'd want to just look around!

For me, the highlight of my spaceflight was going out and spacewalking around the Hubble Space Telescope. We were up at 350 miles—that's a very high altitude for a shuttle flight—and we could see the curvature of the planet from up there. The Earth was so compelling. It was incredible, going outside and being able to spacewalk and look around.

I think about the spacewalks the Apollo astronauts did on the way back from the moon. They had a chance to look in one direction and see a big moon and look in the other direction and see a big Earth.

So I would like to do a moonwalk and look around a little bit out there. It's cool to be inside of the spaceship, but to get outside and walk around… I think that's a very different thing.

The world collectively held its breath as *Apollo 11* touched down on the lunar surface. Onlookers crowded around televisions and radios eager for updates. Do you think any space exploration event since then has reached that level of engagement? When will we have our next "Apollo moment?"

No, I don't think anything has come close, and I don't think anything will come close for hundreds of years. Even if we put someone on Mars, it's not going to be the same. There's only one first time you can leave your planet behind and go to another world. But that's okay. I think the next thing that could get this sort of attention is when—and I think it is *when* and not *if*—we find life somewhere else. That's going to be the next big story.

Print Citations

CMS: Leman, Jennifer. "Q&A: Shuttle Astronaut Mike Massimino on the Legacy of Apollo 11." In *The Reference Shelf: New Frontiers in Space,* edited by Micah L. Issitt, 90-94. Amenia, NY: Grey House Publishing, 2019.

MLA: Leman, Jennifer. "Q&A: Shuttle Astronaut Mike Massimino on the Legacy of Apollo 11." *The Reference Shelf: New Frontiers in Space,* edited by Micah L. Issitt, Grey Housing Publishing, 2019, pp. 90-94.

APA: Leman, J. (2019). Q&A: Shuttle astronaut Mike Massimino on the legacy of Apollo 11. In Micah L. Issitt (Ed.), *The reference shelf: New frontiers in space* (pp. 90-94). Amenia, NY: Grey Housing Publishing.

"A Thrill Ran Through Me": Your Memories of the Apollo 11 Moon Landing

By Matthew Holmes and Guardian Readers
The Guardian, July 19, 2019

'I remember feeling an almost physical thrill run through me'

I was 16 years old, sitting in our huge downstairs recreation room with my parents, my brothers and sister, and many of our closest friends. We were one of the few families with a large colour television in our circle of friends, so we invited many of them to join us to watch Apollo 11 land. As I recall now, there were almost 30 of us sitting and standing, hardly daring to even talk as we watched.

I remember feeling an almost physical thrill run through me as we watched Neil Armstrong climbing down the ladder, and I remember my mother gasping aloud "That was perfect!," through her tears of joy and excitement after he made that famous "That's one small step for a man..." statement. I remember my grandfather screaming with excitement: "Do you believe what we just saw? My lord, can you believe it?" As a young man, he had witnessed Glenn Curtis fly the first airplane over New York and now he'd watched men walk on the moon. He was like a little boy again for a few moments, so delighted to have lived to see both. **Edwin Green, Knoxville, Tennessee, USA**

'We stuck our heads out to stare at the moon—every household in the street was doing the same'

We watched the landing on TV in our shared house in London and as soon as Armstrong stepped out my flatmate and I rushed to the window in the loft and stuck our heads out to stare at the moon—as if we could see him—to find that just about every household in the street was doing the same. It was a great shared moment not just for the street but for mankind. **Carolyn, 73, Bristol**

'I was thrilled beyond belief when I received the crew photo'

We didn't have a television in our home in Delhi so we heard the news via All India Radio. After that and reading all about it in the Times of India, I remember sending a postcard (with my mother's help) to Mr. Neil Armstrong, Apollo 11, NASA, Houston, Texas, USA requesting an autographed photograph.

I was thrilled beyond belief when I received the crew photo with a set of autographs. As a 10-year-old I believed the signatures to be "real"—while an elder in the family said they were rubber stamps. Regardless, it made quite a buzz in school and at home. I was later inspired to become an electrical engineer—the closest thing to the moon I got was working briefly at Caltech's Jet Propulsion Laboratory in Pasadena, where we developed the specifications for what is now the International Space Station. **Krishnaswamy Venkatesh Prasad, Michigan**

'Somehow we thought landing on the moon would make the world a better place'

I watched ghostly black and white images on the TV in my parents' sitting room, with Patrick Moore talking us through things. My father went to bed leaving strict instructions he should be woken when the astronauts emerged. In between the landing and them stepping onto the surface I went outside: the moon was shining brightly and though I couldn't see, I knew the rocket was safely up there. It was the most important, exciting, momentous event of our generation.

We watched breathless as Armstrong climbed down the ladder. We all cried! Somehow we thought landing on the moon would make the world a better place. **Marlene Fenton, Lancashire**

'These have resisted for 50 years, surviving multiple house moves'

My sister and I were sleeping over at an uncle and aunt's place near Lisbon so we could watch the landing and the first walk. I vividly recall Armstrong's first step, all the more exciting having been woken at close to 4am! I had been following space exploration for a couple of years, driven by the contagious excitement and immense knowledge of a friend of my parents who had been an aeronautical engineer, and who later sent me this bundle of newspapers and clippings.

These have resisted for 50 years, surviving multiple house moves through four different countries! Time to frame them now to celebrate this anniversary. **Luis Bernay, Portugal**

'I can't see Apollo 11 take off now without crying—anything was possible'

I had just cancelled my wedding, which should have taken place two weeks later, so my friends were taking me away to help get over it. I can't see Apollo 11 take off now without crying, as it was such an amazing event—but also to me meant freedom and that anything was possible. It was wonderful to be able to lose myself in such an awe-inspiring and beautiful other world. I was lucky enough to later interview James Irwin, who drove the moon buggy for Apollo 15—sitting next to one of the few people who have actually stood on the moon is one of the highlights of my life. **Janet Whitaker, Gloucestershire**

'The whole school marched into assembly to pray for their safe return'

It was just before the summer holidays of my last year at primary school when the astronauts set off for the moon, and I remember the whole school being marched into the assembly hall to pray for their safe return. We were asked to remember the astronauts' children, who were "just like us."

I was so affected by the thought that while Armstrong and Buzz Aldrin were on the moon, Michael Collins was all alone in the command module in the dark and the silence. I thought of him on the dark side and, having been nervous about changing schools, made up my mind that if he was brave enough to do that, I would be fine taking the bus by myself.

> Somehow we thought landing on the moon would make the world a better place.

On the morning they landed my dad woke me up at 3.30am. He held my hand and told me that all people on Earth were making history—I could feel the enormity. **Debbie Brook, Surrey**

'He'd lived through flight by the Wright brothers, to see the moon landings—a giant step'

I watched on a black and white TV in our new home in West Yorkshire, with my father, who'd woken me up to share it with him. We were both huge aviation and space enthusiasts, and I eventually joined the RAF, but we were totally enthralled by the Apollo programme.

We both loved *Tomorrow's World*, and my memories of the moon landings are of James Burke's superb broadcasts. The slide here was issued by the *Daily Express*—and bequeathed to me from my granddad after he died in 1970. He'd lived through flight by the Wright brothers, to see the moon landings—a giant step! **Ian Stacey, Dalkeith**

My dad tells me that my memory is false'

My family had emigrated from India in 1967 and we were living in Wolverhampton. I was four years old and remember sitting in my father's lap, him smelling of whiskey and cigarettes, in the "best" room of our house watching the Eagle land and Armstrong stepping onto the surface of the moon. My strongest memory of the landing is feeling immensely close to my father, and feeling absolutely awestruck by what I was seeing. I knew something stupendous was happening, but I didn't have the words to express my feelings.

My dad tells me we didn't own a TV in 1969 and that my memory is false. I guess he must be right, but my feelings of love for him were so strong at that moment I am choosing to believe my version. **Deepak Puri, 54, Sheffield**

'I was upset because it was "my" party!'

I was six and my birthday was on the day, so we had a special Apollo party with a rocket cake. I remember little, just vague memories of being led into the house to watch TV at some point. My dad was excited, but my strongest memories were that it was quite emotional: I was upset because it was "my" party and I wasn't getting all the attention! Clearly still demanding attention today: I might make a cake on Saturday. **Neil, Northamptonshire**

'I was almost in tears as I berated my mother for letting me sleep!'

I had posters of the astronauts and cosmonauts next to George Best and Bobby Charlton on my walls, Saturn V and Vostok model rockets I had painstakingly made and painted. I loved science fiction films and here was a real live event as fantastic as any film I had seen.

I was nine and had to beg my very pregnant mother to let me watch the whole mission unfold. I struggled to keep my eyes open as I sat on the sofa, and eventually succumbed before waking with a start. "Did they land?" "Yes they did." In that moment I knew I had missed the greatest moment in history! I was almost in tears as I berated my mother for letting me sleep.

My brother was born on July 27 and has Neil in his name. I will be celebrating his birthday in Canada along with the other events of that month 50 years ago, Mum will be there too! **Peter Devine, Manchester**

The contrast between my immobility and the astronauts seemed so unfair'

I was nine and in Stoke Mandeville hospital, having fractured my left femur in a freak swimming pool accident. In those days, treatment consisted of eight weeks in traction with a system of pulleys to straighten the leg.

With nothing to do I became obsessed with Apollo. For the landing itself, the nurses wheeled my bed, pulleys and weights (the furthest I'd moved for weeks!) so that I could see the ward's tiny distant TV in the wee small hours (whether allowed or not). The contrast between my immobility and the apparently unconstrained freedom of the astronauts seemed extraordinarily unfair! Not good enough at maths, I didn't become a space engineer, but a cardiologist instead. The sight of those grainy pictures still brings me out in goose pimples. **Andrew Clark, North Ferriby**

Print Citations

CMS: Holmes, Matthew, and Guardian Readers. "'A Thrill Ran Through Me': Your Memories of the Apollo 11 Moon Landing." In *The Reference Shelf: New Frontiers in Space,* edited by Micah L. Issitt, 95-99. Amenia, NY: 'Grey House Publishing, 2019.

MLA: Holmes, Matthew, and Guardian Readers. "'A Thrill Ran Through Me': Your Memories of the Apollo 11 Moon Landing." *The Reference Shelf: New Frontiers in Space,* edited by Micah L. Issitt, Grey Housing Publishing, 2019, pp. 95-99.

APA: Holmes, M., & Guardian Readers. (2019). "A thrill ran through me": Your memories of the Apollo 11 Moon landing. In Micah L. Issitt (Ed.), *The reference shelf: New frontiers in space* (pp. 95-99). Amenia, NY: Grey Housing Publishing.

The Mission That Changed Everything

By Robin McKie

The Guardian, November 29, 2008

It has proved to be the most enduring image we have of our fragile world. Over a colourless lunar surface, the Earth hangs like a gaudy Christmas bauble against a deep black background. The planet's blue disc—half in shadow—is streaked with faint traces of white, yellow and brown while its edge is sharply defined. There is no blurring that might be expected from the blanket of oxygen and nitrogen that envelops our planet. Our atmosphere is too thin to be seen clearly from the Moon: a striking reminder—if we ever needed one—of the frailty of the biosphere that sustains life on Earth.

This is Earthrise, photographed by astronaut Bill Anders as he and his fellow Apollo 8 crewmen, Jim Lovell and Frank Borman, orbited the Moon on Christmas Eve, 1968. His shot, taken 40 years ago next month, has become the most influential environmental image, and one of the most reproduced photographs, in history. Arguably, his picture is also the most important legacy of the Apollo space programme. Thanks to this image, humans could see, for the first time, their planet, not as continents or oceans, but as a world that was 'whole and round and beautiful and small,' as the poet Archibald MacLeish put it.

Certainly, Earthrise is a striking reminder of Earth's vulnerability. We may have forgotten the men who risked their lives getting to the Moon and who explored its dead landscape—a 'beat-up' world as they put it—but the view they brought back of that glittering blue hemisphere continues to mesmerise.

'Our planet is a lonely speck in the great enveloping cosmic dark,' the US astronomer, Carl Sagan, noted. 'There is no hint that help will come from elsewhere to save us from ourselves.' The opinion is shared by Sir David Attenborough. 'I clearly remember my first sight [of the Earthrise photograph]. I suddenly realised how isolated and lonely we are on Earth.'

Indeed, says the UK space historian Robert Poole, the first popular expressions of ecological concern can be traced to the publication of that picture: dazzling blue ocean, the jacket of cloud and the relative invisibility of the land and human settlement. 'It is a rebuke to the vanity of humankind,' says Poole. 'Earthrise was an epiphany in space.'

In fact, NASA [the National Aeronautics and Space Administration] had not intended to fly to the Moon in 1968. Its lunar hardware was still unproven and Apollo

8 was slated merely to test equipment in low Earth orbit. However, that autumn, the agency was told, incorrectly, by the CIA that the Soviet Union was preparing its own manned lunar mission. So the Apollo programme—established to fulfil President John Kennedy's call for a US manned lunar landing by the end of the decade—was accelerated and Apollo 8 designated for a journey to the Moon, though there would no lander to take men to the lunar surface. That would come on later missions.

The decision was controversial. 'NASA's giant Saturn V rocket, the only launcher capable of taking men to the Moon, had been bedevilled by flaws and instrument failures on its two test flights. Worse, there had been the fire in 1967 in which three astronauts—Gus Grissom, Ed White and Roger Chaffee—were burned to death during a ground test of an Apollo capsule. Sending Lovell, Anders and Borman in an almost identical spacecraft to the Moon, on an unsafe launcher, was a gamble, to say the least.

As a result, most press conferences in the run-up to the launch were dominated by questions about the risks the astronauts faced and, although the mission turned out to be a success, and surpassed all subsequent Apollo missions for the precision of its flight path and lack of glitches, it was dogged at the start by control-room nerves and tension.

Finally, at 6.31am, on Saturday 21 December, the Saturn V—at 360 ft, the tallest, most powerful rocket ever built and for the first time carrying a human crew—blasted Borman, Anders and Lovell into space. The launch was shattering. 'The Earth shakes, cars rattle and vibrations beat in the chest,' as Anne Morrow Lindbergh, the writer and wife of the aviator Charles Lindbergh put it.

In the event, the rocket performed perfectly and put Apollo 8 safely into orbit. Using a 'state-of-the-art' computer—which had less power than a modern hand calculator—Lovell keyed in the commands that fired the launcher's third stage and sent their craft hurtling on its three-day journey to the Moon. The spaceship had become the first manned vehicle to slip the surly bonds of Earth and head to another world.

The outward trip was not without its mishaps. As the astronauts settled down for their first night in space, cramped into a craft the size of a minivan, they found it difficult to sleep. So Borman tried a sleeping pill. This was a mistake. A couple of hours later, he was struck by a fit of vomiting and diarrhoea, a tricky affliction in zero gravity, as Robert Zimmerman recalls in *Genesis: The Story of Apollo 8*. 'Borman, Lovell and Anders found themselves scrambling about the cabin, trying to capture blobs of faeces and vomit with paper towels. So much for the glamour of space flight.' Certainly, it was an inelegant way to travel to another world.

Early on Christmas Eve, Apollo 8 reached its destination. The astronauts fired the craft's Service Propulsion System (SPS) rocket to slow as it swept past the Moon and the little ship slipped into lunar orbit. For its first three revolutions, the astronauts kept its windows pointing down towards the Moon and frantically filmed the craters and mountains below. Reconnaissance for subsequent Apollo landings was a key task for the mission.

It was not until Apollo 8 was on its fourth orbit that Borman decided to roll the craft away from the Moon and to point its windows towards the horizon in order to get a navigational fix. (The capsule's astronauts still used sextants to guide their craft.) A few minutes later, he spotted a blue-and-white fuzzy blob edging over the horizon. Transcripts of the Apollo 8 mission reveal the astronaut in a rare moment of losing his cool as he realised what he was watching: Earth, then a quarter of million miles away, rising from behind the Moon. 'Oh my God! Look at the picture over there. Here's the Earth coming up,' Borman shouts. This is followed by a flurry of startled responses from Anders and Lovell and a battle—won by Anders—to find a camera to photograph the unfolding scene. His first image is in black-and-white and shows Earth only just peeping over the horizon. A few minutes later, having stuffed a roll of 70mm colour film into his Hasselblad, he takes the photograph of Earthrise that became an icon of 20th-century technological endeavour and ecological awareness.

In this way, humans first recorded their home planet from another world. 'It was,' Borman later recalled, 'the most beautiful, heart-catching sight of my life, one that sent a torrent of nostalgia, of sheer homesickness, surging through me. It was the only thing in space that had any colour to it. Everything else was either black or white. But not the Earth.' Or as Lovell put it, our home world is simply 'a grand oasis'.

Last week, I spoke to Lovell, now a vigorously healthy 80-year-old and owner of the Lovells of Lake Forest restaurant in northern Chicago, where his son, Jay, is chef. An experienced astronaut even before he flew on *Apollo* 8, he achieved his greatest fame as commander of the ill-fated *Apollo 13* mission—which only narrowly survived a fuel-tank explosion en route to the Moon in 1970. (Lovell was played by Tom Hanks in Ron Howard's film, *Apollo 13*, in 1995.) 'Apollo 8 was a high point for me without a doubt. Apollo 13 was certainly less pleasant. It was touch and go, after all.' Nor does he fail to appreciate the importance of that photograph. 'The predominant colours were white, blue and brown,' he recalled. 'The green of the Earth's grassland and forests is filtered out by the atmosphere and appears as a bluish haze from space.' The effect is to give Earth an added, especially intense blue veneer.

'Bill [Anders] had the camera with colour film and a telephoto lens,' he said. 'That is what makes the picture. Earth is about the size of a thumbnail when seen with the naked eye from the Moon. The telephoto lens makes it seem bigger and gives the picture that special quality.' (Seven months later, Neil Armstrong—standing on the lunar surface—also noted he could blot out the Earth with his thumb. Did that make him feel really big, he was asked years later? 'No,' the great astronaut replied, 'it made me feel really, really small.')

The Earthrise photograph became an icon of 20th-century technological endeavor and ecological awareness.

By Christmas Day, the whole world had become engrossed in Apollo 8's epic journey: 1968 had been a particularly traumatic year and the planet was desperate for a diversion. In the US, Robert Kennedy and Martin Luther King had been assassinated, the Vietnam War had worsened dramatically and civil and student conflict was spreading through US cities. In Europe, the Prague 'spring' had been crushed by Soviet tanks. People needed cheer and the realisation that humans had reached the Moon provided that uplift perfectly.

There was a further twist to the mission's timing. Stanley Kubrick and Arthur C. Clarke's visionary epic *2001: A Space Odyssey* was then showing in cinemas round the globe. (The Apollo 8 crew had attended its Houston premiere three months earlier.) The film ends with the embryonic Star Child hanging in space above the Earth: a tiny, glittering blue disc very like the one that had just been pictured by Anders. The links between Apollo 8 and *2001* went further than that, however. The film depicts space travel as commonplace and there, to prove the accuracy of its vision, were men orbiting the Moon. It seemed to many people—including myself, then a university student and a space-programme devotee—that all those dreams of science fiction writers and film-makers might soon be realised. It was a wondrous Christmas.

Indeed, it can be fairly claimed that Apollo 8 was the real Man on the Moon story. By the time, Armstrong and Buzz Aldrin reached the Moon on Apollo 11, the world had already got used to the idea of manned lunar flight. By contrast, Apollo 8 took many people unawares. Certainly, you could easily argue that it, and not Apollo 11, deserves the title of the greatest event of the 20th century. Lovell believes that. 'I sat beside Charles Lindbergh at the launch of Apollo 11. "It's a great event," he said, "but you know you were the ones who really spearheaded the moon programme."'

Anders, Borman and Lovell orbited the Moon 10 times. Then, as they prepared to head back to Earth, the astronauts held a last televised press conference. Each then took turns to read out the first 10 verses of the book of Genesis as they skimmed, at a height of 70 miles, over the lunar surface. The Old Testament struck many people as an odd choice for a final lunar reading. But all three (at the time, at least) were deeply religious: Borman and Lovell were Protestants, Anders a Catholic. None of them saw any ambiguity in reading out a version of creation that was at complete odds with the version supported by the scientists who had got them there. In any case, the reading went down well in America.

A few hours later, Lovell fired the SPS engine again and Apollo 8 began its homeward journey, splashing down in the Pacific on 27 December. As the astronauts waited to be picked up by the navy, 10ft waves pounded their craft. Borman, once again, was sick. Apart from that, their homecoming was a triumph.

After that, Anders' colour film was processed and passed to the media. *Time* ran the photograph with single word 'Dawn' while *Life* published a lengthy display of images from the mission, including a poster-sized spread of the Earthrise photograph.

Seven months later, Apollo 11 reached the lunar surface. It was the beginning of the end for space programme. Three years later, Apollo 17 lifted off from the Moon, the last human visit to this dead world. The US public, who had funded the programme, tired of the Moon and turned to concerns closer to home. 'Looking back, it is possible to see that Earthrise marked the tipping point, the moment when the sense of the space age flipped from what it means for space to what it meant for Earth,' says Robert Poole in his recent book *Earthrise: How Man First Saw the Earth.*

Humans had spent billions in an attempt to explore another world and in the end rediscovered their own. It was a point stressed by Apollo 17 astronaut Harrison Schmitt, one of the last men on the Moon. 'Like our childhood home, we really see the Earth only as we prepare to leave it,' he wrote.

However, of all the efforts to sum up the story of Earthrise, the best is made by T.S. Eliot in last of the Quartets:

'We shall not cease from exploration
And the end of all our exploring
Will be to arrive where we started
And know the place for the first time.'

Additional research by Hermione Hoby

Fly me to the moon: The three astronauts who made history

Jim Lovell
Apollo 8 pilot (later commander of Apollo 13)

Like his Apollo 8 companions, Jim Lovell came from a modest background. He was born on 25 March, 1928, the son of a Philadelphia coal furnace salesman who died when Lovell was 12. As a result, Lovell had to rely on a US navy scholarship to see him through university. He served in the Korean War before becoming a navy test pilot and then a NASA astronaut in 1962. He flew on two Gemini missions before Apollo 8. Of its three crewmen, Lovell was the only one to return to space—as commander of Apollo 13. Thus he became one of only three men to travel twice to the Moon. Gene Cernan (on Apollos 10 and 17) and John Young (on Apollos 10 and 16) are the others. However, of this trio, Lovell was the only one who never made it to the surface. Although he was scheduled to land with Apollo 13, a fuel tank explosion forced its crew to abandon their landing and to struggle back to Earth. Today, Lovell helps run the Lovells of Lake Forest restaurant near Chicago, where his son, Jay, is chef, and raises money to help young students study science and become involved in the US space programme.

Bill Anders
Apollo 8 pilot

The son of a US navy lieutenant, Anders was born in October 1933 and grew up in San Diego, California, before becoming a jet pilot, joining the Apollo programme in 1963. Apollo 8 was his only space mission, though he can claim to have made as great an impact as any other seasoned space traveller on that trip: his image of Earthrise has become the environmentalists' icon. The mission affected him profoundly. Once a devout Catholic, he found his experience of space made a mockery of his beliefs and he gave up religion. Anders served in a number of senior US government offices before becoming CEO of General Dynamics. He retired in 1994.

Frank Borman
Apollo 8 commander

Born on 14 March 1928, Borman was brought up in Tucson, Arizona, and after graduating from West Point, served as a fighter pilot before becoming a US air force test pilot and then an astronaut in 1962. After Apollo 8, Borman left NASA, joined Eastern Air Lines and eventually became its CEO in December 1975. Borman retired from the airline in 1986. He now lives in Las Cruces, New Mexico, where he rebuilds and flies Second World War and Korean War aircraft.

Print Citations

CMS: McKie, Robin. "The Mission That Changed Everything." In *The Reference Shelf: New Frontiers in Space,* edited by Micah L. Issitt, 100-105. Amenia, NY: Grey House Publishing, 2019.

MLA: McKie, Robin. "The Mission That Changed Everything." *The Reference Shelf: New Frontiers in Space,* edited by Micah L. Issitt, Grey Housing Publishing, 2019, pp. 100-105.

APA: McKie, R. (2019). The mission that changed everything. In Micah L. Issitt (Ed.), *The reference shelf: New frontiers in space* (pp. 100-105). Amenia, NY: Grey Housing Publishing.

Apollo 13: Lessons from the Successful Failure

By Geoff Loftus
Forbes, April 3, 2013

On April 11, it will have been forty-three years since the Apollo 13 lunar mission became one of the greatest death-defying adventures in history. Three astronauts, mission commander Jim Lovell, Fred Haise, and Jack Swigert, found themselves rocketing around the moon in a pair of joined vehicles, each with the interior space of a VW Beetle, almost no power, and no heat. As one of the supervisors at Mission Control in Houston said, "Not a good way to fly."

A little more than two days into the mission, the service module's No.2 oxygen tank exploded, and No.1 tank failed as well; collateral damage from the explosion. The result: all three men "abandoned" the command module (CM) for the close confines of the lunar module (LM). The LM was intended for two men (Lovell and Haise) to use in their landing on the lunar surface and then their return to the command module. It wasn't designed or built to be used extensively by three men, but Apollo 13's crew had no other options.

As the history of the mission on the NASA website says: "Ground controllers in Houston faced a formidable task. Completely new procedures had to be written and tested in the simulator before being passed up to the crew. The navigation problem had to be solved; essentially how, when and in what attitude to burn the LM descent engine to provide a quick return home. "

As anyone who has seen the incredible movie *Apollo 13* knows, one of the biggest challenges of the mission was making course corrections. For an incredible five minutes, Lovell and Haise fired the LM's engines (never designed for this kind of navigational burn) and used the sun as a point of navigational alignment. The alignment with the sun proved to be less than .5 degrees off. At 73 hours, 46 minutes into the mission, the air-to-ground transcript describes the event:

Lovell: OK. We got it. I think we got it. What diameter was it?

Haise: Yes. It's coming back in. Just a second.

Lovell: Yes, yaw's coming back in. Just about it.

Haise: Yaw is in....

Lovell: What have you got?

Haise: Upper-right corner of the sun....

Lovell: We've got it! If we raised our voices, I submit it was justified.

Flight Director Gerald Griffin, a man not easily shaken, recalled: "Some years later I went back to the log and looked up that mission. My writing was almost illegible, I was so damned nervous. And I remember the exhilaration running through me: My God, that's the last hurdle—if we can do that, I know we can make it. It was funny because only the people involved knew how important it was to have that platform properly aligned."

This astounding piece of flying was done under insane conditions: not only were Lovell and Haise using equipment not designed for the purpose, they were doing it without proper food (without power, the crew couldn't heat anything, and all three men skipped meals) and with a severe lack of sleep—with most of the electrical systems turned off, the spacecraft's temperature dropped to 38 degrees Fahrenheit and condensation formed on all the walls.

As NASA's site says, "The most remarkable achievement of mission control was quickly developing procedures for powering up the CM after its long, cold sleep. Flight controllers wrote the documents for this innovation in three days, instead of the usual three months."

Using those procedures, Swigert and Lovell powered up the command module, and Apollo 13 splashed down safely in the Pacific on April 17, 1970.

The mission was almost immediately dubbed a "successful failure"—a failure since it never achieved its prime objective of landing on the moon. Successful because almost every single person who worked for NASA pulled together in an astounding feat of teamwork to save the crew. As Fred Haise said in an interview with CBS News, "We had to have Plan B's and C's and D's and on and on." Hundreds of people in Mission Control refused to fail and did whatever they had to do to give Apollo 13 its Plan B's, C's, and D's.

> Almost every single person who worked for NASA pulled together in an astounding feat of teamwork to save the crew.

What Are the Leadership Lessons from Apollo 13's Successful Failure?

Prioritize and Communicate—NASA didn't worry about anything other than saving the crew. The lunar landing objective was abandoned within minutes of the initial explosion. And everyone on the gigantic NASA team understood it.

Experience Takes Experience—There's no substitute for hours and hours of actually doing something. It's the best preparation for catastrophe. NASA's people had been in the lunar-landing business for 9 years when the explosion occurred aboard Apollo 13.

Training is the Next Best Thing—There are things you can't experience until they happen. But you can run simulations and training exercises. NASA trained and trained and trained. (My brother was in the U.S. Navy and once told me about the harsh conditions under which sailors were trained to fight shipboard fires. I was astounded. But the one time he had to fight a major fire aboard ship, he and every other sailor fell right into doing the things they had been trained to do. The fire was extinguished and no one got hurt.)

Assess and Manage Risk—When you are doing something as risky as sending people in sealed containers attached to explosives into space, you'd better have pretty darn good risk management techniques. NASA had to adjust on the fly (pun intended) during Apollo 13, but many of its improvisations were worked out in advance because NASA had done a good job of identifying many of its risks.

I had the privilege of meeting Jim Lovell soon after the movie *Apollo 13* came out in 1995. He was doing a speaking tour, usually to business audiences, about the kinds of things I mentioned above. Lovell is a rare creature: a true American hero. He's funnier, cooler, more attractive, and braver than the movie star who played him in the movie. (I bet Tom Hanks would be the first person to agree with me on that.) At the time of the Apollo 13 mission, Lovell was America's No. 1 pilot—he'd been in space more often than anyone else and still is the only man to travel to the moon twice.

According to his book, *Lost Moon*, as Apollo 13's capsule landed in the ocean and the astronauts saw water running down the outside of their portholes, Lovell quietly pronounced the end of the successful failure: "Fellows, we're home."

Print Citations

CMS: Loftus, Geoff. "Apollo 13: Lessons from the Successful Failure." In *The Reference Shelf: New Frontiers in Space,* edited by Micah L. Issitt, 106-108. Amenia, NY: Grey House Publishing, 2019.

MLA: Loftus, Geoff. "Apollo 13: Lessons from the Successful Failure." *The Reference Shelf: New Frontiers in Space,* edited by Micah L. Issitt, Grey Housing Publishing, 2019, pp. 106-108.

APA: Loftus, G. (2019). Apollo 13: Lessons from the successful failure. In Micah L. Issitt (Ed.), *The reference shelf: New frontiers in space* (pp. 106-108). Amenia, NY: Grey Housing Publishing.

4
NASA and the International Space Station

By NASA.

This image of an aurora was taken by astronaut Christina Koch from aboard the International Space Station. She said of the image, "Years ago at the South Pole, I looked up to the aurora for inspiration through the 6-month winter night. Now I know they're just as awe-inspiring from above."

Space Futures

For years, budget cuts and diminished political interest have slowed the pace of development in American space science. Progress today is far shy of the goals that leaders in the field imagined during the Apollo Program of the 1960s and 70s, when politicians and scientists alike imagined that astronauts would long since have reached Mars. In 2019, NASA administrators, scientists, and politicians are struggling to define the future of space science for the next generation, and coping with questions concerning how to manage America's investment in the International Space Station (ISS) and future space habitat programs, the future of NASA exploratory missions, and about the future of manned versus automated space exploration.

NASA's Future

The Apollo Program, which began in the 1960s and ended in the 1970s, was initially far more ambitious than what NASA was able to accomplish. Had the Apollo Program not ended in the late 1970s, it might have continued for decades, developing capabilities through a continuing series of launches and manned missions. Instead, even before the famed *Apollo 11* mission that landed Neil Armstrong and Buzz Aldrin on the Moon, the program had suffered budget cuts and decreased support among the legislature. *Apollo 11* had, for many American citizens and politicians alike, satisfied their interest in the program, based on two major factors: achieving the goal that President Kennedy set in the early 1960s; and beating the Russians to that goal. However, although many Americans were satisfied that the Space Race had come to its natural conclusion, NASA scientists saw the *Apollo 11* mission as just the most comprehensive test of their system. The H-Class missions that followed, which included *Apollo 12*, *Apollo 13*, and *Apollo 14*, were the beginning of a series of advanced missions. Even the "successful failure" of *Apollo 13* proved that the crews, both in space and on the ground, had reached a level of expertise signifying enormous future potential.

Following *Apollo 11*, the Nixon administration faced pressure to cut funding to NASA, resulting in serious cutbacks to planned missions. The decision to end the Apollo Program in 1972 saw the loss of millions of dollars in investments in both equipment and operational experience. The new Space Shuttle Program that took its place was favored by politicians because the idea of a new space program generated more news coverage and, thus, more political leverage to take advantage of during campaigning. This route, however, set back space exploration to a place from which it has never fully recovered. President Lyndon B. Johnson, who supported the Apollo Program as a Senate majority leader in 1958, predicted the fate that befell the program, as the first round of budget cuts reached the White House. He famously stated in 1967, "The way the American people are, now that they have all this capability, instead of taking advantage of it, they'll probably just piss it all away."[1]

In the 1980s, just before the collapse of the Soviet Union, President Ronald Reagan and former USSR chief Mikhail Gorbachev had a series of meetings in Moscow in which they discussed the possibility of a collaborative Russian-U.S. mission to Mars. The collapse of the USSR and fickle political attitudes in the United States prevented this from happening. Mars exploration, however, has remained a major priority for NASA scientists, who gained scientific knowledge of the planet with a series of unmanned robots that explored and returned data from Mars. The most famous was the Opportunity Rover, which landed on the surface of Mars in 2004 and was active until 2018, when NASA lost contact with the rover. The formal end of the program was announced in 2019.

Some NASA officials believe that Mars should remain the organization's primary focus. Former astronaut Michael Collins said, in interviews about the 50th anniversary of the first moonwalk, that NASA should not focus on additional moonwalks, which he feels will detract from the ultimate goal, the exploration of Mars, adding that missions to Mars are still likely a long way off.[2] For NASA, manned missions to Mars have taken a backseat to other, easier-to-achieve goals. As of 2019, NASA is planning to resume landings on the Moon by 2024, this time exploring the Moon's South Pole. Meanwhile, at NASA's Jet Propulsion Laboratory (JPL), plans are being made for a new Mars rover to continue the robotic exploration of Mars, and for a variety of new instruments to enhance telescopic and data gathering projects ongoing at NASA and associated research organizations.[3] Potential future plans include a mission to use automated technology to explore Europa, an icy moon orbiting the planet Jupiter where there is believed to be a salty ocean beneath layers of ice.[4]

Fueling NASA's new era will be a new generation of space vehicle, similar to the Apollo mission craft used in the 1960s and 70s. NASA's next generation space vehicles are groundbreaking in that they have been designed and constructed by private companies or through a public-private partnership. In 2017, NASA unveiled its first new passenger vehicle since the retirement of the Space Shuttle program, a new space plane called the *Dream Chaser*. This plane, designed by the space tourism division of the Sierra Nevada Corporation,[5] hopes to enable astronauts to dock with the International Space Station (ISS). As of 2019, NASA also has the Lockheed Martin-designed *Orion* Multi-Purpose Crew Vehicle, designed to carry passengers out of Earth's orbit and, eventually, as the first passengers to Mars.[6] Also in the works at NASA are new autonomous flying vehicles designed to conduct unmanned space exploration missions.

NASA's *Dream Chaser* and *Orion* were completed through a public-private partnership and, as America edges into an era of private space travel, this may come to be a more familiar model for space exploration and science. The excitement surrounding the idea of space tourism becoming a reality has, in fact, led some industry analysts to speculate that the United States might be on the verge of a new space age, though the exact form that this will take remains uncertain.

Old Technology

In 2018, President Donald Trump's administration announced plans to defund America's financial commitment to the ISS. The aging orbiting facility has been the site of numerous diplomatic meetings between astronauts, has hosted some of the world's first space tourists, and has been an enduring symbol of international cooperation. The space station, which was scheduled to remain in orbit for 15 years, has been orbiting the earth for more than 20. The Obama administration weighed plans to bring the ISS back to Earth in a controlled crash, but instead continued its funding. The Trump administration is proposing that the United States sell its shares in the international facility by 2025, basically privatizing it.[7] The proposal met with political opposition and criticism by economists, who warned that it was not economically beneficial. It is, however, similar in the approach used to cancel the Apollo Program and replace it with the Space Shuttle Program, which favored new programs over the continuation or rehabilitation of existing ones. Creating new programs can draw public and media attention and provide a political advantage.[8]

Whatever politicians decide with regard to the fate of the ISS, many see the future of space station technology will likely be in the hands of private companies. Several of the companies now in this arena are not only investing heavily in the emerging space tourism industry, but also in plans to build their own space stations, where tourists can dock, engage in space walks, and observe the Earth and Moon from orbit. Some are experimenting with cutting-edge technology for construction and maintenance processes. One company has proposed using a series of space robots to build a functional habitat for scientists, tourists, or even colonists. Other companies are experimenting with automated machines that can use 3D printing technology to create needed parts in space, rather than launching equipment and materials into space from the earth's surface. NASA is also experimenting with the possibility of using automation and robotics to construct facilities in space for astronauts visiting the Moon or Mars. However, though research into future space station technology is ongoing at NASA, it is downplaying that aspect, hoping to benefit from the surge in private investment and commercial research. Meanwhile, NASA will concentrate its limited governmental revenues on the organization's primary goals: returning astronauts to the moon and preparing for the first manned missions to Mars.[9]

A New Space Age

The flurry of private investment brought about by the dawn of the space tourism industry has helped to reinvigorate public interest in space flight and technology, which some have called a new Space Age in America. However, consequences of a space age dominated by private investment are yet to be determined. Privatization can increase productivity, because companies are motivated to aggressively develop toward the goal of profiting from their investment. Further, competition between companies can increase innovation as companies search for new features to give them a competitive advantage in their field. The private market thereby encourages development, investment, and innovation, but depending on how this market is managed, the free market can also stifle development and innovation. This occurs as some of the companies become leaders in the industry and then use their economic power to influence legislation or to suppress competition. Ultimately, the best possible product available to consumers is not the result of a completely free market, but of regulation and management to ensure that companies are not able to block competition to the point of disadvantaging consumers.

Enabling private space companies to lead the way means that much of the development will be guided by profit, which does not always benefit consumers. As of 2019, the cost of the most basic space tourism package available is in the realm of $50 million, which means that the commercial activity is aimed at an extremely small audience of uber-wealthy consumers. Of course, companies will most likely seek to lower costs to appeal to a broader consumer base, but such development will be profit-oriented and aimed at a far different niche than publicly funded scientific programs and projects.

Because NASA is publicly funded, its data belongs to the American public. NASA scientists therefore have an obligation to consider public welfare both when choosing topics for research and when determining how to disseminate data to the public. For example, NASA scientists have led the field in climate research and provided legitimate data to the public on the nature and progress of climate change. By contrast, corporations, who function for the benefit of employees and shareholders, have funded and produced fake research to obfuscate data on climate change so they can remain free to exploit the earth's natural resources in ways that exacerbate the problem. While the privatization of space promises to become an extremely lucrative industry and is already stimulating engineering breakthroughs that will fuel the next wave of space travel and science, it is important to understand the difference between development and research undertaken for public welfare and that undertaken for profit.

Works Used

Brinkmann, Paul. "U.S. Should Skip Moon, Head for Mars, Apollo 11's Michael Collins Says." *UPI*. Jul 15, 2019. Retrieved from https://www.upi.com/Top_News/US/2019/07/15/US-should-skip-moon-head-for-Mars-Apollo-11s-Michael-Collins-says/5701563151864/.

"Europa Lander." *JPL*. NASA Jet Propulsion Laboratory. 2019. Retrieved from https://www.jpl.nasa.gov/missions/europa-lander/.

Howell, Elizabeth. "Orion Spacecraft: Taking Astronauts Beyond Earth Orbit." *Space*. Nov 20, 2018. Retrieved from https://www.space.com/27824-orion-spacecraft.html.

Pappalardo, Joe. "A 10-Year Odyssey: What Space Stations Will Look Like in 2030." *Popular Mechanics*. Jun 10, 2019. Retrieved from https://www.popularmechanics.com/space/satellites/a27886809/future-of-iss-space-station/.

Portree, David S. "Dreaming a Different Apollo." *Wired*. Oct 13, 2014. Retrieved from https://www.wired.com/2014/10/dreamingadifferentapollo/.

Powell, Corey S. "The ISS Was Never Supposed to End Like This." *MACH*. NBC News. Feb 22, 2018. Retrieved from https://www.nbcnews.com/mach/science/iss-was-never-supposed-end-ncna848771.

Rinehart, Will. "The Options for the Future of the International Space Station." *American Action Forum*. Sep 25, 2018.

Tamblyn, Thomas. "NASA Unveils Its First Spaceplane Since the Shuttle." *Huffington Post*. Aug 25, 2017. Retrieved from https://www.huffingtonpost.co.uk/entry/nasa-unveils-its-first-spaceplane-since-the-shuttle_uk_59a01123e4b0821444c29987?guccounter=1.

"The Future." *NASA*. 2019. Retrieved from https://www.nasa.gov/specials/60counting/future.html.

Notes

1. Portree, "Dreaming a Different Apollo."
2. Brinkmann, "U.S. Should Skip Moon, Head for Mars, Apollo 11's Michael Collins says."
3. "The Future," *NASA*.
4. "Europa Lander," *JPL*.
5. Tamblyn, "NASA Unveils Its First Spaceplane Since the Shuttle."
6. Howell, "Orion Spacecraft: Taking Astronauts Beyond Earth Orbit."
7. Powell, "The ISS Was Never Supposed to End Like This."
8. Rinehart, "The Options for the Future of the International Space Station."
9. Pappalardo, "A 10-Year Odyssey: What Space Stations Will Look Like in 2030."

What's Next for NASA?

By Brian Dunbar
National Aeronautics and Space Administration, January 31, 2019

NASA's vision: We reach for new heights and reveal the unknown for the benefit of humankind.

Thousands of people have been working around the world—and off of it—for decades, trying to answer some basic questions. What's out there? How do we get there? What will we find? What can we learn there, or learn just by trying to get there, that will make life better here on Earth?

Explore our history, see who we are and how we work, check the list of current missions, and find out what we're launching next. Here's a look at some of the big things coming up.

Solar System and Beyond

NASA will add to its existing robotic fleet at the Red Planet with the InSight Mars lander set to study the planet's interior. The Mars 2020 rover will look for signs of past microbial life, gather samples for future return to Earth and investigate resources that could someday support astronauts.

The James Webb Space Telescope will be the premier observatory of the next decade, studying every phase in the history of our Universe in infrared, while the Parker Solar Probe will "touch the sun," travelling closer to the surface than any spacecraft before.

NASA's first asteroid sample return mission, OSIRIS-REx, arrives at the near-Earth asteroid Bennu in August 2018, and will return a sample for study in 2023.

Launched in April 2018, the Transiting Exoplanet Survey Satellite (TESS) will search for planets outside our solar system by monitoring 200,000 bright, nearby stars.

And a mission to Jupiter's ocean-bearing moon Europa is being planned for launch in the 2020s.

Sending Humans Out into Solar System: Moon to Mars

Building on this growing scientific knowledge of our solar system, NASA is developing the most advanced rocket and spacecraft to lead the next steps of human exploration farther into space than we have ever traveled before. Launching from a revitalized NASA Kennedy Space Center in Florida, the agency's powerful Space

Launch System rocket will carry astronauts aboard NASA's Orion spacecraft to the Moon, where astronauts will build and begin testing the systems needed for challenging missions to other destinations, including Mars, and deeper into space.

NASA will test its new deep space exploration system beginning with an integrated, uncrewed flight of SLS and Orion, known as Exploration Mission-1. During the second and subsequent early flights, NASA will develop new technologies and techniques and apply innovative approaches to solving problems in preparation for longer-duration missions far from Earth. NASA will build up its deep space capabilities before ultimately sending humans to the Red Planet.

International Space Station

Humans are already living and working off the Earth in the one-of-a kind research laboratory in microgravity. The International Space Station serves as a blueprint for global cooperation and scientific advancements, a destination for growing a commercial marketplace in low-Earth orbit, and a test bed for demonstrating new technologies. Research on the station is the springboard to NASA's next great leap in exploration, sending humans into deep space.

> By studying astronauts living in space for six months or more, NASA is learning how future crews can thrive on longer missions farther into the solar system.

A new generation of U.S. commercial spacecraft and rockets are supplying cargo to the space station and will soon launch astronauts once again from U.S. soil.

By studying astronauts living in space for six months or more—including two who were there for nearly a year—NASA is learning how future crews can thrive on longer missions farther into the solar system. The space station also is a test bed for exploration technologies like autonomous refueling of spacecraft, advanced life support systems and human/robotic interfaces.

A portion of the astronauts' time aboard the space station has been designated for national laboratory investigations that provide direct benefits to improve life on Earth, and NASA is committed to using this unique resource for wide-ranging scientific research.

Flight

NASA is helping transform aviation by developing advanced technologies for revolutionary aircraft shapes and propulsion, and for the airspace in which they fly, which dramatically improve efficiency, reduce noise and maintain safety in more crowded skies.

NASA is working now to design, build and fly new experimental aircraft—X-planes—that will prove the dramatic benefits of advanced technologies in piloted flight, including a Low Boom Flight Demonstrator which will provide data that could open the door to supersonic flights over land.

Space Tech

On Earth and in space, NASA is developing, testing and flying cutting-edge technologies for a new future of human and robotic exploration. Technology development at NASA provides the onramp for new space technologies, creating a pipeline that matures them from early-stage through flight.

We'll continue to evolve technologies like advanced solar electric propulsion, deep space navigation, new green propellants, and in-space manufacturing and assembly. These new space technologies will advance NASA's capabilities to help us reach our future deep space destinations.

Earth

NASA brings together technology, science, and unique global Earth observations to provide societal benefits and strengthen our nation. Critical to understanding how our planet's natural resources and climate are changing, our observations form the foundation for important environmental planning and decisions by people all over the world.

In 2018, NASA will launch the next generation of two missions—ICESat-2 and GRACE Follow-On—to continue the long-term record of how Earth's ice sheets, sea level, and underground water reserves are changing.

Print Citations

CMS: Dunbar, Brian. "What's Next for NASA?" In *The Reference Shelf: New Frontiers in Space,* edited by Micah L. Issitt, 117-119. Amenia, NY: Grey House Publishing, 2019.

MLA: Dunbar, Brian. "What's Next for NASA?" *The Reference Shelf: New Frontiers in Space,* edited by Micah L. Issitt, Grey Housing Publishing, 2019, pp. 117-119.

APA: Dunbar, B. (2019). What's next for NASA? In Micah L. Issitt (Ed.), *The reference shelf: New frontiers in space* (pp. 117-119). Amenia, NY: Grey Housing Publishing.

What Space Stations Will Look Like in 2030

By Joe Pappalardo
Popular Mechanics, June 20, 2019

The International Space Station, one of the history's engineering marvels, is still under NASA management. The effort to cut funding has never succeeded, but the $4 billion annual price tag of supporting the station is sapping efforts to put an American flag on Mars. So the aging station's life won't be extended, which makes engineering *and* economic sense—even politicians can't argue against gravity and metal fatigue.

However, the seeds of a new industry are being planted onboard. The clearest sign of this is the space hotel prototype attached to the station's Harmony module. Inside, a pair of company engineers is performing a shakedown flight to validate the design. The idea is not to remain an annex to ISS, but to fly the hardware on its own and become a free-flying, for-profit destination.

There are exterior and interior experiment racks for researchers, and for tourists, there are big windows and doublewide sleeping bags suitable for an orbital honeymoon. Inside the ISS, a visitor is ready to arrive. A few years ago, this person had no reasonable method to explore space, but when the rules changed in 2019, this wealthy actor/musician snatched up a round trip ticket having no compunction about putting $50 million down for a week in space.

The celebrity floats past a rack of experiments, not sparing them a look. Inside is the largest protein crystal grow-out ever attempted in orbit. Studying individual protein molecules is extremely difficult because they are so small. However, clever researchers have figured out that growing a crystal from protein molecules will create a repeating array that can reveal the molecular structure. So if they know the protein's exact structure, they can design medicine with it.

There are several projects ongoing inside the racks, aimed at unraveling Parkinson's disease, finding antidotes to toxic agents, and developing immunotherapy for cancer. These projects preceded 2019, but kicked into higher gear since the for-profit research limits have been lifted.

There's an economy of scale here: the experiment racks have been made larger and optimized by a space research company and so several interested pharma companies have cost-shared space on a private space flight to the station. The astronauts are still needed to run the experiments, but the space research company has automated the process as much as possible.

The research done in space is having an impact back home. There are manufacturing innovations being invented here that couldn't be discovered on Earth: perfect microscopic spheres (courtesy of a lack of surface tension) for encapsulating drugs, fiber optic glass with unprecedented smoothness and speed of transmission, and ultra-thin sheets of gallium arsenide that can be used in semiconductors.

along with these experiments, there's a 3d printer in a box attached to the hull. Its robotic arm is plying layers of material on a long lattice frame. These are solar panels, being made in space where they will also be used. The more surface area, the more power can be collected, but launch vehicles can't fit such long, flat structures in their vehicles. That's where those complex, folding solar arrays come in. But making panels in space enables optimized sizes and removes the risk of a malfunction when the array unfolds. Simple is always better.

SpaceX and Boeing continue sending astronauts skyward (and reap the public rewards for delivering astronauts and famous people to the station), but its the new generation of manufacturing breakthroughs that will really change everything.

It's the end of the road for ISS.

As the world watches, mission controllers order the final commands that push the space station into a fatal plunge. It's taken two years (and nearly a billion dollars in fuel) to position the ISS just right to guide it into the Pacific Ocean. This is the most remote spot on the planet. They call it "Point Nemo," and it's become a spacecraft graveyard.

And there will be a big splash. NASA estimates that somewhere between 53,500 and 173,250 pounds of space station will dropping into the ocean.

It's the end of ISS, but it has spawned a new generation of stations that even now are in orbit. These have spent time attached to ISS but are now free-flying, self-sustaining space stations. There are about 5 private space stations flying in 2030, not including the Chinese outpost.

These are no cookie cutter copies of ISS, or even of each other. These myriad platforms are built and operated by various people, whether public-private partnerships or commercial operations populated by researchers trying to maximize microgravity. Other stations have berths for space tourists, but very few aggressively focus on ferrying the super rich to low-earth orbit (LEO). There's good money and less risk in flying scientists.

And these activities will be open to the world, so nations with some money but not enough to have their own space stations are renting rides and space for their own research priorities. Places like Nigeria, South Korea, and the United Arab Emirates now have turnkey space programs, complete with national astronauts, science projects, and commercial research.

There are more of these "sovereign astronauts" than there are space tourists as the reality of the experience—cramped, constipated, and costly—is starting to set into these well-heeled adventurers.

Very few (if any) of this new crop of space stations are populated full-time. Private space modules are built with automation in mind, fewer skilled repairs, and no orbital spacewalks. In fact, most run without anyone on board at all, keeping them ready for visitors or tending to long duration experiments. Robot arms affixed to walls tend to the manual work when human beings are absent. There is also an emerging market for space station repair, which is an offshoot of the satellite servicing business that's booming in LEO as a growing number of constellations encircle the globe.

These space stations look similar. They each have prominent solar arrays, communication antenna, and emergency escape capsules. They are each smaller by far than ISS ever was, but are built for different purposes: Blue Origin's station is a repurposed rocket, making for a long, slender station. With twin solar panels, the entire thing is shaped like a T. Lockheed Martin's looks like a mini ISS, with the station wedged between flat, wide solar panels. And Axiom's space station looks like a mushroom.

Some of these stations are busy proving just how far orbital construction can go. The most ambitious is a private firm that's creating small satellites in space. It's easier and cheaper to fly the needed materials into space than finished parts. A 3D printer in orbit takes those raw materials and churns out small sats, available to create or fill holes in existing constellations.

This effort is neat but not as impressive as the other major orbital construction project — a handful of spider-like robot spacecraft creating struts and other long structural parts for a new space habitat. Smaller stations, lower launch costs, and in-orbit construction are what define this new generation of space exploration.

But where is NASA in all of this? The space agency has handed the reins to LEO to private companies, but the agency is still pouring money into crewed deep space missions with its eyes continually set on Mars. But government funding is going further

> **Other stations have berths for space tourists, but very few aggressively focus on ferrying the super rich to low-earth (LEO) orbit.**

since they can now piggyback off the private sector's progress, and there are the obvious savings associated with having spaceflight competition.

t's a replay of the way NASA seeded the development of the SpaceX, Grumman, and Boeing commercial launch vehicles, which in turn enabled all of this action in orbit in the first place. By loosening their grip on LEO, NASA has seeded an economic infrastructure that can exist without its direct funding.

With NASA focused on Mars, commercial entities start floating ideas of their own lunar bases. If there's a market for science, tourism, or industry (water mining, solar panel construction or the like), it will be private space companies building the hardware and managing the missions on their own—after they enable NASA to land there.

By the time the year ends, there's talk of establishing a wholly private base on the moon. Finally, tourists will have a destination and scientists will have a base to plumb the Moon's many mysteries.

And it's this lunar colony that marks a major transition in human history—the first steps off Earth and toward a multi-planetary species. The new space stations in orbit are now seen as the first baby steps to this future, a step first taken in 2019.

Now, the solar system awaits.

Print Citations

CMS: Pappalardo, Joe. "What Space Stations Will Look Like in 2030." In *The Reference Shelf: New Frontiers in Space,* edited by Micah L. Issitt, 120-123. Amenia, NY: Grey House Publishing, 2019.

MLA: Pappalardo, Joe. "What Space Stations Will Look Like in 2030." *The Reference Shelf: New Frontiers in Space,* edited by Micah L. Issitt, Grey Housing Publishing, 2019, pp. 120-123.

APA: Pappalardo, J. (2019). What space stations will look like in 2030. In Micah L. Issitt (Ed.), *The reference shelf: New frontiers in space* (pp. 120-123). Amenia, NY: Grey Housing Publishing.

As NASA Aims for the Moon, an Aging Space Station Faces an Uncertain Future

By Nell GreenfieldBoyce

NPR, July 7, 2019

When a rocket carrying the first module of the International Space Station blasted off from Kazakhstan in November of 1998, NASA officials said the station would serve as an orbiting home for astronauts and cosmonauts for at least 15 years.

It has now been more than 18 years that the station has been continuously occupied by people. The place is impressive, with more living space than a six-bedroom house and with two bathrooms and a large bay window for looking down at Earth.

NASA and its international partners have spent decades and more than $100 billion to make the station a reality. The trouble is, as the agency sets its sights on returning people to the moon, the aging station has become a financial burden. And it's not clear what its future holds.

NASA spends between $3 billion and $4 billion a year operating the station and flying people back and forth. That's about half the agency's budget for human exploration of space.

The United States and other participating nations have pledged to fund the space station until at least 2024, but it will surely last longer than that. Gilles Leclerc, head of space exploration at the Canadian Space Agency, says there's no way that the international partners would come together in five years and decide to just crash the station into the ocean so that resources could be directed to other space goals.

"It would be a waste. We cannot ditch the International Space Station. There's just too much invested," Leclerc says. "It's quite clear, it's unanimous between the partners that we continue to need a space station in low Earth orbit."

So NASA has floated one money-saving idea: Turn the space station over to the private sector. That's why, a few weeks ago, NASA officials held a big press event at the Nasdaq stock market's MarketSite in New York City.

"NASA is opening the International Space Station to commercial opportunities and marketing these opportunities as we've never done before," said the agency's chief financial officer, Jeff DeWit. "The commercialization of low Earth orbit will enable NASA to focus resources to land the first woman and next man on the moon by 2024, as the first phase in creating a sustainable lunar presence to prepare for future missions to Mars."

Astronaut Christina Koch appeared in video beamed down from space. "We are so excited to be part of NASA as our home and laboratory in space transitions into being accessible to expanded commercial and marketing opportunities, as well as to private astronauts," she said.

All this produced a sense of déjà vu in John Logsdon, a space historian with George Washington University. In the 1980s, when Ronald Reagan's administration first proposed building a permanent space station, part of the pitch was "the idea that it could be a place for a wide variety of commercial activities, with billions of dollars of economic payoff," says Logsdon. "So here we are in 2019, finally going to test that hypothesis."

When reporters asked how much revenue could come in from new commercial activities on the station, however, NASA officials wouldn't give any numbers, saying there was too much uncertainty.

"The 12 industry studies NASA commissioned last year estimated revenue projections for future low-Earth orbit destinations across a variety of markets, and those projections varied significantly as a result of uncertainty

> **If the space station became commercially operated or even privately owned, NASA could become just one of many customers.**

associated with these future markets," a NASA spokesperson told *NPR*. "The markets and services that will generate revenue need to be cultivated by the creative and entrepreneurial private sector."

"That is the right answer because they don't know yet," says Tommy Sanford, executive director of the Commercial Spaceflight Federation.

But if the space station became commercially operated or even privately owned, NASA could become just one of many customers.

"You need to be focused on adding as many customers as possible and hoping to reach a tipping point, at some point, where you retain all of them," says Sanford. "Then that eventually lowers your cost, because you are one of many customers. You aren't bearing the entire cost of the infrastructure and transportation."

Some question whether any business could make a go of running a space station without the government still ponying up a ton of money.

"Candidly, the scant commercial interest shown in the station over its nearly 20 years of operation give us pause about the agency's current plans," NASA Inspector General Paul Martin told members of Congress last year.

As all of these discussions go on, the station keeps getting older. Space is a harsh environment. The hardware is wearing out, and major components are certified only until 2028.

"Space station really has up to, say, less than 10 years of lifetime," says Dava Newman, a scientist at MIT and a former NASA deputy administrator.

She loves the station and has flown experiments on it. But she thinks with time running out, there needs to be a strategic plan for its end.

"There might be some elements of space station that the private [sector] might be able to take over, a module or two," she says. "All of that needs to be put into place, probably with government funding."

Eventually, big components of the station will have to crash back down to Earth. Asked when NASA expected to deorbit the station, a spokesperson for the agency said that no specific year is being targeted.

"Transition from the space station will occur once commercial habitable destinations are available and can support NASA's needs as one of many customers," the spokesperson said.

Print Citations

CMS: Greenfieldboyce, Nell. "As NASA Aims for the Moon, an Aging Space Station Faces an Uncertain Future." In *The Reference Shelf: New Frontiers in Space,* edited by Micah L. Issitt, 124-126. Amenia, NY: Grey House Publishing, 2019.

MLA: Greenfieldboyce, Nell. "As NASA Aims for the Moon, an Aging Space Station Faces an Uncertain Future." *The Reference Shelf: New Frontiers in Space,* edited by Micah L. Issitt, Grey Housing Publishing, 2019, pp. 124-126.

APA: Greenfieldboyce, N. (2019). As NASA aims for the Moon, an aging space station faces an uncertain future. In Micah L. Issitt (Ed.), *The reference shelf: New frontiers in space* (pp. 124-126). Amenia, NY: Grey Housing Publishing.

How Americans See the Future of Space Exploration, 50 Years after the First Moon Landing

By Courtney Johnson
Pew Research Center, July 17, 2019

This week marks the 50th anniversary of the Apollo 11 moon landing, which was the first time humans set foot on the moon. The United States remains the only country to have put people on the moon, and, as of 2018, the large majority of Americans consider it essential that the U.S. continue to be a leader in space exploration. However, many Americans do not think future manned trips to the moon—or to Mars—should be a high priority for NASA. Instead, they put higher priority on other roles such as monitoring Earth's climate or asteroids that could hit Earth.

Here are six Pew Research Center findings about Americans' views of space travel.

1. Most Americans think sending astronauts to Mars or the moon should be a lower priority for NASA—or say it should not be done at all. While a majority of Americans (58%) said in a 2018 survey that human astronauts are essential to the future of the U.S. space program, less than one-in-five describe sending human astronauts to Mars (18%) or the moon (13%) as *top* priorities for NASA. Americans are more likely to rate these goals as "important but lower priorities" (45% and 42%, respectively), or to say they are not important or should not be done at all (37% and 44%).

NASA has not put a human on the surface of the moon since the Apollo 17 mission in 1972. But just last month, NASA announced plans to put the first woman on the moon in 2024 as part of the Artemis program. The program also aims to put human beings on the surface of Mars by the 2030s.

2. Americans see priorities other than a moon or Mars landing as more pressing for NASA. About six-in-ten (63%) say one of the organization's top priorities should be using space to monitor key parts of Earth's climate system. About four-in-ten or more said other top priorities should include conducting basic scientific research to increase knowledge of space (47%) and developing technologies that could be adapted for other uses (41%).

3. Half of Americans think space travel will become routine during the next 50 years of space exploration. Private companies like Virgin Galactic and SpaceX have plans to take tourists on suborbital space flights in the future. NASA also recently announced that it would open the International Space Station up for tourists. For now, these trips will be prohibitively expensive for the average person— for example, Virgin Galactic's tickets cost about $250,000, and NASA estimates one trip to the space station would cost about $58 million. Still, half of Americans expect space travel to become routine by 2068.

However, even if space travel does become commonplace, more than half of Americans (58%) say they would *not* be interested in going. People who aren't interested in orbiting the Earth in a spacecraft cite a number of concerns, including thinking it would be too expensive or scary or that their health or age would not allow for safe travel. Among the 42% who would be interested, the most common reason is that they want to experience something unique.

4. A majority of Americans say the U.S. must remain a global leader in space exploration, and that NASA's continued involvement is essential. The large majority of Americans (72%) say it is essential that the U.S. continue to be a world leader in space exploration; just 27% say it is not essential. This sentiment is shared equally across generations and among Republicans and Democrats.

A majority of Americans (65%) also describe NASA's continued involvement in space exploration as essential. Another 33% say that private companies will ensure that enough progress is made in space exploration, even without NASA's involvement. Democrats and Democratic-leaning independents (70%) are more likely than Republicans and Republican-leaning independents (59%) to say NASA must continue playing a role in space exploration. Conversely, Republicans (41%) are more likely than Democrats (28%) to say private companies will ensure that enough progress is made.

> The large majority of Americans (72%) say it is essential that the U.S. continue to be a world leader in space exploration. Half of Americans expect space travel to become routine by 2068.

5. Americans have little confidence that private space companies will minimize space debris. Just 13% of Americans say they have a great deal of confidence that private space companies will minimize the amount of human-made space debris that they put into Earth's orbit—including fragments of rockets, satellites and other human-made objects. About half (51%) of Americans say they have not too much or no confidence at all that private companies will minimize the debris they create.

Space debris, sometimes called "space junk," is a growing concern. NASA estimates that more than 23,000 pieces of space debris 10 centimeters or larger are orbiting the Earth, and these objects could damage important spacecraft like the International Space Station.

While Americans are skeptical that private companies will limit the debris they create, they are more confident that these firms will make a profit: 44% say they have a great deal of confidence that companies like SpaceX, Blue Origin or Virgin Galactic will do this, and another 36% say they have a fair amount of confidence.

6. Americans are not enthusiastic about the idea of creating a military Space Force. The U.S. Department of Defense has long had satellites orbiting Earth, and the notion of a larger American military presence in space has been around since the 1960s. While President Donald Trump has talked about creating a Space Force as an entirely new branch of the military, most members of the public are not on-board with this plan: A May 2019 Pew Research Center survey found 36% of Americans approve of creating a military Space Force, while 60% disapprove. U.S. military veterans are more evenly split on this idea, but still more disapprove (53%) than approve (45%).

Print Citations

CMS: Johnson, Courtney. "How Americans See the Future of Space Exploration, 50 Years after the First Moon Landing." In *The Reference Shelf: New Frontiers in Space*, edited by Micah L. Issitt, 127-129. Amenia, NY: Grey House Publishing, 2019.

MLA: Johnson, Courtney. "How Americans See the Future of Space Exploration, 50 Years after the First Moon Landing." *The Reference Shelf: New Frontiers in Space*, edited by Micah L. Issitt, Grey Housing Publishing, 2019, pp. 127-129.

APA: Johnson, C. (2019). How Americans see the future of space exploration, 50 years after the first Moon landing. In Micah L. Issitt (Ed.), *The reference shelf: New frontiers in space* (pp. 127-129). Amenia, NY: Grey Housing Publishing.

NASA Seeks to Break the "Tyranny of Launch" with In-Space Manufacturing

By Eric Berger

Ars Technica, July 29, 2019

Made in Space is one of the most intriguing companies in aerospace because it's not so much focused on getting into space. Rather, the company is focused on doing interesting, meaningful, and potentially profitable things once there. Its long-term goal is to build factories in space using additive manufacturing.

A recent NASA contract, worth $73.7 million, will allow Made in Space to significantly accelerate those efforts. "For us, this is one of those watershed moments that take this technology and propel it into the next stage," said Andrew Rush, president and chief executive officer, in an interview with *Ars*. Made in Space started the year with 40 employees and will end it with nearly 100.

The NASA contract will fund the company to build and fly a spacecraft it calls Archinaut One, with the aim of constructing two 10-meter solar arrays in orbit. These two arrays will power an ESPA-class satellite. (These are fairly small satellites, about 200 kg, that are typically carried as secondary payloads by large rockets such as the Falcon 9 booster built by SpaceX.)

> Instead of a few hundred watts of power, therefore, a small satellite might be able to have as much as five to eight times that amount to work with.

The basic idea is that, if Archinaut One can manufacture its own solar arrays in space—rather than having to fold them in a cumbersome way inside a payload fairing—they can be much larger than those on a typical ESPA-class satellite. Instead of a few hundred watts of power, therefore, a small satellite might be able to have as much as five to eight times that amount to work with.

Typically, such power capabilities have only been available on much larger satellites flying in geostationary space. More electricity will allow satellite operations to use significantly more powerful sensors, on-board computing, and more, Rush said.

Made in Space has already performed some ground-based demonstrations of the Archinaut technology, which manufactures a central spar onto which rolled up solar arrays can be extended and locked into place. The NASA funding will allow Made in Space to build the spacecraft, test it on the ground, and then fly it into space. The company is targeting a 2022 launch on an Electron booster built by Rocket Lab.

Importance of Space Technology

NASA funded the demonstration mission through its Space Technology Mission Directorate. This part of NASA, which is distinct from the agency's other programs, funds the kinds of breakthrough technologies that may not be of immediate use but are the seed corn for cutting-edge exploration in one or two decades.

"In-space robotic manufacturing and assembly are unquestionable game-changers and fundamental capabilities for future space exploration," said Jim Reuter, associate administrator of NASA's Space Technology Mission Directorate. "By taking the lead in the development of this transformative technology, the United States will maintain its leadership in space exploration as we push forward with astronauts to the Moon and then on to Mars."

For Made in Space, this is an important step toward breaking the "tyranny of launch," by which every mission that leaves Earth is constrained by its dimensions, including size, mass, and its ability to survive the dynamic forces of launch. By manufacturing satellite components in space, the company hopes to unfetter some of those launch constraints.

Print Citations

CMS: Berger, Eric. "NASA Seeks to Break the 'Tyranny of Launch' with In-Space Manufacturing." In *The Reference Shelf: New Frontiers in Space,* edited by Micah L. Issitt, 130-131. Amenia, NY: Grey House Publishing, 2019.

MLA: Berger, Eric. "NASA Seeks to Break the 'Tyranny of Launch' with In-Space Manufacturing." *The Reference Shelf: New Frontiers in Space,* edited by Micah L. Issitt, Grey Housing Publishing, 2019, pp.130-131.

APA: Berger, E. (2019). NASA seeks to break the "tyranny of launch" with in-space manufacturing. In Micah L. Issitt (Ed.), *The reference shelf: New frontiers in space* (pp. 130-131). Amenia, NY: Grey Housing Publishing.

NASA Chooses Saturn's Moon Titan as Its Next Destination

By Mary Beth Griggs
The Verge, June 27, 2019

A new mission involving a drone-like lander will explore the surface of Saturn's moon Titan. The mission—called Dragonfly—received a coveted funding slot from NASA's New Frontiers program, which funds ambitious missions to explore objects in our Solar System.

"Dragonfly is a Mars rover-sized drone that will be able to fly from place to place on Titan," Elizabeth "Zibi" Turtle, the lead investigator of the mission, said in a briefing. The 10-foot-long, and 10-foot-wide dual-quadcopter will look like a giant drone, with eight rotors helping it soar across the moon's surface for about 8 or 9 miles (12-14 kilometers) in under an hour. It will make one of these "hops" about once every 16 days, scouting out future landing sites, spending a lot of time sampling the surface, and observing the weather. It will also be able to make shorter hops of just a few feet if the scientists spot something interesting near a landing site.

On Titan, it's actually easier for a vehicle to fly than to roll in order to get to all the different places that the scientists would like to explore. Titan's gravity is just a seventh of Earth's and the atmosphere is four times thicker than our planet's. That makes it perfect for flying. "If you put on wings, you'd be able to fly on Titan," Turtle says.

Dragonfly was one of two finalists being considered for the New Frontiers award. The other, CAESAR, led by Steve Squyres at Cornell University, would have aimed to grab a piece of a comet's surface and bring it back to Earth. "For the comet sample return mission unfortunately the race is over." Thomas Zurbuchen, NASA's Associate Administrator for the Science Mission Directorate said during a press conference. But he also added that other funding opportunities would open up in the future. "Some of the best ideas take multiple shots on goal before they become a reality," he said.

The two missions had already made it through several competitive rounds before the final decision. New Frontiers missions generally cost around $850 million to develop, making them slightly pricier than the agency's Discovery missions, like the Mars InSight lander, which cost about $814 million, or the Dawn spacecraft which cost $500 million.

Only three other missions have been funded through the New Frontiers program. The Juno spacecraft, in orbit around Jupiter, has been observing the giant planet's roiling atmosphere and magnetic field. New Horizons wooshed by Pluto in 2015, and flew by a Kuiper Belt object in December of 2018. And OSIRIS-REx, an asteroid-sampling mission, is currently in orbit around the asteroid Bennu, looking for a safe place to grab a sample next year.

Like those missions, Dragonfly is expected to expand our view of distant objects in the solar system—in this case, Saturn's moon Titan, whose bizarre chemistry and thick atmosphere have intrigued scientists for years. (It is the only moon in our system to boast a substantial atmosphere.) The Huygens probe, carried by Cassini, gave us a first glimpse of the moon's surface. Then, Cassini itself

> **Titan's gravity is just a seventh of Earth's and the atomosphere is four times thicker than our planet.**

revealed that Titan had lakes of liquid methane on the surface—making it the only other body in our Solar System to boast substantial bodies of liquid on its surface besides Earth. Dragonfly's ability to travel across the surface will let researchers visit several interesting sites over the course of the planned two-year mission, traveling about 108 miles (175 kilometers) during that time.

Its first target will be a soft sea of sand dunes that offers a safe landing site. Turtle describes them as "Basically the largest Zen gardens in the Solar System wrapped around almost the entire equatorial region." From there, Dragonfly, powered by a nuclear generator and onboard batteries, will eventually make its way to Selk crater, taking pictures and samples along the way.

The spacecraft will be loaded with scientific equipment. The researchers are interested in Titan's geology (could there be ice volcanoes or Titanquakes?) but they're also *really* interested in its chemistry. Like any mission to another world, they'll be looking for evidence of life, but they'll also be interested to see how these chemicals interact on their own. Those observations could give us a window into how similar materials might have interacted on Earth before life developed here.

"Titan is just a perfect chemical laboratory to understand prebiotic chemistry— the chemistry that occurred before chemistry took the step to biology," Turtle says. "Ingredients that we know are necessary for the development of life as we know it are sitting on the surface of Titan." Those ingredients include organic molecules on the surface, sunlight and evidence of water hanging out on the surface in the past. All of those factors come together in Selk crater, making it a tantalizing science destination.

Dragonfly is set to launch in 2026 and won't land on Titan until 2034, so we'll have to wait a long time to get our first images of the mission's insect-eye view of another world.

Correction 6/29: This story has been updated to clarify that Titan and Earth are currently the only bodies in the Solar System known to have substantial liquid on their surface—liquid has been found in other places in the solar system, often buried beneath the surface.

Print Citations

CMS: Griggs, Mary Beth. "NASA Chooses Saturn's Moon Titan as Its Next Destination." In *The Reference Shelf: New Frontiers in Space,* edited by Micah L. Issitt, 132-134. Amenia, NY: Grey House Publishing, 2019.

MLA: Griggs, Mary Beth. "NASA Chooses Saturn's Moon Titan as Its Next Destination." *The Reference Shelf: New Frontiers in Space,* edited by Micah L. Issitt, Grey Housing Publishing, 2019, pp. 132-134.

APA: Griggs, M.B. (2019). NASA chooses Saturn's moon Titan as its next destination. In Micah L. Issitt (Ed.), *The reference shelf: New frontiers in space* (pp. 132-134). Amenia, NY: Grey Housing Publishing.

With Opportunity Lost, NASA Confronts the Tenuous Future of Mars Exploration

By John Wenz
Smithsonian, February 20, 2019

Things are changing on Mars. For two decades, NASA has regularly launched missions to the planet, engaging in a sustained effort of robotic exploration. These missions have revealed signs of water, complex organic compounds, volcanic activity and tantalizing hints of possible life—either extinct and gone, or, perhaps, lurking in the subterranean realms of the planet to this very day.

Since the dawn of the 21st century, NASA has successfully sent eight spacecraft to Mars, to orbit or to land, with no failures. But looking into the future, a marked lack of NASA missions to the planet breaks a pattern that has persisted for decades.

"We're taking for granted this incredible presence NASA has had for 20 years, and we're watching that wither away," says Casey Dreier, chief advocate and senior space policy adviser at the Planetary Society, an NGO co-founded by Carl Sagan in 1980 to advocate space science and exploration.

In the near term, the Martian landscape will see no lack of robotic activity. The InSight lander touched down on the surface of the planet last November. Just last week, NASA announced that the Opportunity rover, which had been exploring Mars for almost 15 years, has finally shut down for good. And as the 2020 launch window for Mars missions approaches, countries around the world are gearing up for interplanetary launches—the most spacecraft to fly for Mars at the same time in history.

After 2020, however, the Mars manifest is conspicuously thin. Without a mission to follow NASA's Mars 2020 rover, many scientists are left wondering what comes next in the reconnaissance of the most accessible and hospitable world beyond our own—a planet that NASA plans to land astronauts on in another 20 short years.

* * * * * * * * * *

Mars and Earth align every 26 months for an ideal launch to the red planet, and not coincidentally, NASA has sent a spacecraft to Mars about every other year on average since 2000. The next launch window opens up in July and August of 2020, with spacecraft expected to arrive at Mars about half a year later.

In 2020, NASA is planning to send a flagship rover—an upgraded version of Curiosity—to the surface of Mars. The European Space Agency (ESA) and Roscosmos are also planning to send a rover, recently named for DNA scientist Rosalind Franklin, to Mars next year. China is planning an orbiter and rover, Japan has an orbiter and lander in the works, and the United Arab Emirates is planning its first Mars orbiter as well—all in 2020. Two more spacecraft from the Indian and Japanese space agencies are slated to follow in 2022 and 2024, respectively.

The most ambitious of these missions is NASA's Mars 2020 (which will receive an official name before launch). While the 2020 rover is still under construction, NASA has taken an important step toward tackling the goals of the mission: selecting a landing site. Jezero Crater, Mars 2020's future home, features a now-dry river delta where steams are thought to have once flowed into a large lake bed.

Jezero Crater has a couple of major aspects that make it very attractive," says Michael Meyer, NASA's Mars exploration lead scientist. "One is that you can look at it and you know it's a delta. The geomorphology is fairly obvious."

Meyer says that evidence from orbiters points to past river flows into the lake basin, transporting materials from all over the planet. As a result, "you have a good assemblage of minerals there."

The geologically rich Jezero Crater makes the dried lake bed an ideal site for one of Mars 2020's primary objectives: to cache samples and deposit them on the surface for a future mission to pick up and launch back to Earth. The problem is that no future mission for sample return currently exists—and for planetary scientists, the idea of gathering samples on Mars and leaving them there indefinitely is simply unpalatable.

"It will begin caching samples for return to the Earth," Dreier says. "The question, though, is if we're going to come get them."

* * * * * * * * * *

It's hard to overstate the value of planetary samples brought back to labs on Earth—and humanity has never returned a sample from Mars. Compared to using a spacecraft's onboard instruments, scientists can measure samples on the ground with much higher precision, revealing such subtle clues as isotope ratios that could provide "smoking gun" evidence of life.

Without a sample return, "you're going to find powder burns," Meyer says. "You're not going to find the gun."

A sample return mission has long been a goal of planetary scientists, tracing its official origins back to at least a 2007 study titled *An Astrobiology Strategy for the Exploration of Mars*.

"It laid out what you needed to do to find out if there was life on Mars," Meyer says. "It essentially came down to: The next step is to do sample returns."

To collect the samples that Mars 2020 leaves on the surface of the planet, NASA is considering multiple mission plans. The leading idea is to use a lander with a small "fetch rover" to grab the samples and then blast them into Mars orbit, where a spacecraft would snag them and fly back home.

Sample return is, "broadly within the scientific community, one of the highest priority scientific goals," Dreier says.

However, the decision to fund such a mission, which Dreier says would likely cost about $2 or $3 billion, is made by Congress, not NASA. The current White House administration, which wields significant influence shaping the direction of NASA, is focused on human exploration of the moon rather than robotic exploration of Mars, even though sending astronauts to Mars is a stated long-term goal.

Within NASA, however, Meyer says there is some inertia toward a sample return mission—mostly in the form of feasibility studies. Optimistically, the space agency could shoot for the 2026 launch window to bring back some of the red regolith of Mars.

After 2020, if NASA does not attempt another launch to Mars until 2026, it will be the longest gap in the space agency's missions to Mars since a hiatus between 1975 and 1992.

****

In the coming decade, NASA may face a more fundamental problem than leaving uncollected samples on the surface of Mars. The primary telecommunications relays between Earth and Mars, Mars Odyssey and the Mars Reconnaissance Orbiter, are around 17 and 13 years old, respectively.

"We know full well that to bank on them being there 20 years from now is silly," Meyer says. "Banking on them being there 10 years from now is more credible."

A proposal for a new orbiting spacecraft to serve as a communications link, called the Next Mars Orbiter, was initially envisioned for a launch in 2022. However, the various and competing needs for a new Mars spacecraft have since scrapped the initial plan. Many scientists want to use the next mission to Mars for sample return, while others argue the need for a communications relay is more im-

To collect the samples that Mars 2020 leaves on the surface of the planet, NASA is considering multiple mission plans.

mediate—and a third option would morph the Next Mars Orbiter into a large-scale mission that could do both, a prospect that would require significant technological advances. In any case, Next Mars Orbiter (or whatever it becomes) seems unlikely to launch until the late 2020s.

NASA has another potential solution, however. Future NASA operations could hitchhike on missions sent by other space agencies. Institutions around the world have Mars ambitions, from countries like India and the United Arab Emirates to private companies like SpaceX.

By cooperating with international and private space institutions, NASA could affordably send CubeSats or other small-scale spacecraft. Such a mission could, in theory, work as a surveyor and science mission for one agency while doubling as a communications relay for NASA.

"We are willing to entertain a different mode," Meyer says. "Instead of buying a spacecraft and having it do x, we actually just buy x and let someone else figure what to do with it."

Mars 2020 is shaping up to be one of the most ambitious planetary exploration missions in history, and it could provide an unprecedented picture of the planet's history, habitability and viability for future human exploration. But the rover will also be collecting priceless samples of Martian material, the true key to unlocking the planet's past—and at the moment, no one knows how we are going to pick them up.

Print Citations

CMS: Wenz, John. "With Opportunity Lost, NASA Confronts the Tenuous Future of Mars Exploration." In *The Reference Shelf: New Frontiers in Space,* edited by Micah L. Issitt, 135-138. Amenia, NY: Grey House Publishing, 2019.

MLA: Wenz, John. "With Opportunity Lost, NASA Confronts the Tenuous Future of Mars Exploration." *The Reference Shelf: New Frontiers in Space,* edited by Micah L. Issitt, Grey Housing Publishing, 2019, pp. 135-138.

APA: Wenz, J. (2019). With opportunity lost, NASA confronts the tenuous future of Mars exploration. In Micah L. Issitt (Ed.), *The reference shelf: New frontiers in space* (pp. 135-138). Amenia, NY: Grey Housing Publishing.

5
Space in Popular Culture

By NASA, via Wikimedia.

Pictured is the test-bed space shuttle *Enterprise*, named after the fictional starship, with *Star Trek* TV show cast members and creator. Left to right: Dr. James C. Fletcher (NASA Administrator), DeForest Kelley (Dr. "Bones" McCoy), George Takei (Mr. Sulu), James Doohan (Chief Engineer "Scotty" Scott), Nichelle Nichols (Lt. Uhura), Leonard Nimoy (Mr. Spock), Gene Roddenberry (show creator), Democratic Congressman Don Fuqua, and Walter Koenig (Ensign Pavel Chekov).

Aliens, Movies, and Fiction

For as long as humanity has existed, space has fueled mythology and fantasy. The flickering lights visible from the surface of the Earth were the source of some of the earliest creation myths, and many of Earth's dominant religions, including Christianity, still incorporate "the heavens" into their metaphysical concepts of existence. From the 25 percent of Americans who believe in horoscopes to the more than 30 percent who believe that extraterrestrial life has visited the planet, space continues to enthrall, inform, and captivate. This potential to fuel spiritualism and imagination exists in an uneasy balance with the emerging scientific understanding of the cosmos.[1] As more realistic images of space matriculate into popular culture, the image of space and humanity's future in space both collides and melds with ancient concepts of the universe beyond Earth.

Belief and Disbelief

For the earliest humans, space was a mystery. Seen only from Earth, the remnants of stars and planets—thousands of years old by the time their traces reached the planet's surface—fueled innumerable theories and fantasies. Some saw lights in the sky as evidence of a cosmic realm beyond the Earth, or of sentient cosmic forces watching over the Earth. The nearest astronomical object, the Moon, fostered a rich lore of its own. The shapes of crevices and craters were seen as evidence of lunar civilizations, or signs that the Moon itself was a living entity (the man in the Moon) spying on the darkened Earth. Early humans recognized that the Moon and stars changed positions, shifting through the hours and seasons. They saw that the Moon was connected to the movement of the tides and to the phases of the year. Space objects were thus linked to the annual cycles of activities that marked the passage of time in human culture and were endowed with spiritual significance.

Over time, mythology became linked with cultural tradition identity. This is one reason why the introduction of science into human society continues to be a violent and controversial process. When Nicolaus Copernicus proposed that the Earth rotated around the sun, the Catholic Church banned his book on the subject, *Des revolutionibus*, for more than 200 years. Another famous early astronomer, Galileo Galilei, was convicted of heresy by the Catholic Church for making similar observations and he was threatened with execution.[2] As the science of astronomy developed, the accumulation of data about the universe was met with institutional resistance by members of churches that wielded military power.

Over time, the advance of science works to dispel myths. This process, however, is arduous and frequently accompanied by resistance from individuals who do not wish to relinquish their world view, which they have come to see as an essential expression of their identity.

Skepticism and resistance to science occurs for a number of reasons. In some cases, individuals resist scientific data because the data in question poses some threat to their livelihood or personal lives. In some cases, individuals prefer the more "spiritual" or "fantastic" explanation over the seemingly more banal scientific explanations.

When the *Apollo* 8 mission provided the first photographs of the Moon and Earth from space, some people refused to believe in the images or their scientific explanations. An antiscience world view was promoted, claiming that scientific data is often the product of a shadowy agenda intended to obfuscate core truths about the universe. Some embrace antiscience because their identity is linked to spiritual principles that are contradicted by scientific data. Others desire to maintain an image of the world suffused with magic and supernatural forces.[3]

Whether or not a person embraces scientific data is also connected to a person's relationship with his or her larger society. The scientific process has been so influential and effective in the advancement of human life, that is has become, in many ways, an official state philosophy, meaning that trust in science is linked to how a person feels about the established socio-political order in their environment and their perception of governmental untrustworthiness.

There is evidence that 30 percent of Americans believe that aliens from other planets have visited the Earth and that the government has not only hidden this fact, but is secretly experimenting on aliens. Others believe that the truth of extraterrestrial life has been hidden to prevent panic. In 2019, a social media campaign called for people to storm a secret government facility, known as Area 51, that has long been depicted in fiction as the site where the government conceals extraterrestrial technology or bodies of extraterrestrial visitors. There is little legitimate evidence to suggest that extraterrestrial visitation has occurred, but Area 51 conspiracy theories are embraced primarily by those with an inherent distrust of their government. This skepticism in science is a rejection not of scientific data, but of the trustworthiness of the persons who act as gatekeepers of scientific data.

From Fiction to Reality

Science fiction and science evolved in concert, with discoveries in science fueling fiction, while fiction likewise fueling development in science. There is a surprisingly long list of scientific inventions that were first imagined in the pages of science fiction literature or films. The possibility of deriving solar energy from space, for instance, was first imagined by famed science fiction novelist Isaac Asimov in 1941, and is in the process of becoming science fact. In other examples, biotechnologists are currently developing artificial skin to cover prosthetic limbs, an idea gleaned from the popular film *The Empire Strikes Back*, while the U.S. military is developing a high-tech armor for soldiers, known as the Tactical Assault Light Operator Suit (TALOS), inspired by the 1968 superhero debut of Marvel Comics' Iron Man. In 2015, scientists in England demonstrated the world's first "tractor beam," a device capable of moving objects at a distance that has been featured in many different science fiction films and novels, and the now largely defunct flip phone takes its inspiration from the flappable communicators used in the 1960s television series *Star Trek*.[4] More recently, scientists have begun working on another invention plucked from science fiction, an elevator that can move objects between Earth and space, an idea popularized by popular science fiction author Arthur C. Clarke in his novel *The Fountains of Paradise*."

The interplay between fiction and scientific research plays a considerable role in the advancement of science, but also colors how individuals imagine science and space. For generations raised in the 1960s, for instance, popular fiction portrayed a twenty-first century in which humanity was at the brink of colonizing space. The fictional images of humans in space have infiltrated deep into American culture, and this manifests in many different ways.

Fiction also reflects and informs popular culture in the depiction of aliens. The earliest television series and films depicting alien life were limited by available special effects technology and budgets, but they also demonstrate the limits of human imagination. Aliens were nearly always (and still typically are) depicted as very humanoid in appearance or resembling some other Earth species. Fiction writers and special effects artists often base non-humanoid aliens on more unusual Earth creatures with a distinctly alien appearance, such as insects or deep sea organisms. Scientists specializing in theories about extraterrestrial life (a field known as exobiology) have stated that given the tremendous variation possible for living organisms, it is unlikely that aliens would resemble humans and that it is quite possible that an alien might not resemble any Earth-bound creature. However, some scientists disagree and argue that the evolution of life in a pattern similar to the way life evolved on Earth may have occurred elsewhere in the universe, making it possible that humanoid aliens exist somewhere in the cosmos.[5] In the 1961 novel *Solaris*, writer Stanislav Lem imagined a first encounter between humanity and an altogether different kind of life, a sentient planet capable of contacting the minds of the humans sent to observe it. This extremely unusual take on alien life reflected what Lem saw as a distinct possibility of such an encounter, that the nature of an alien consciousness would be so different and alien from human experience that it would ultimately be impossible to interpret or understand.

One of the most lasting imagined depictions of aliens is as "little green men," small, green, hairless humanoid beings with large almond-shaped eyes and thin, long appendages. Some researchers in the field of science fiction now believe that this image came from the era before science fiction itself, and was ultimately derived from Western European folklore and specifically versions of a story called the "Green Children of Woolpit," depicting strange events surrounding the arrival of two green children in a little village. The first known science fiction story to cast aliens as small, green creatures was the story "Mayaya's Little Green Men," from an issue of *Weird Tales* published in 1946 and written by author Harold Lawlor. Soon after, other authors utilized similar depictions of aliens, and the little green men trope became familiar in American popular culture.[6]

The origin of this trope reflects the changing role that fiction literature played in human culture as scientific knowledge gradually permeated the popular imagination.

The earliest depictions of alien life drew more from the realm of fantasy, depicting aliens as strange and bizarre creatures whose appearance and behavior was largely unfathomable. Depictions of alien life in this vein expresses the ancient human fear and amazement at the wonders of the universe, the same imaginative substrate that gave rise to stories of gods and mythological heroes in every culture around the world. While some scientists believe that unfathomable aliens might actually be closer to reality, the depiction of aliens as strange, otherworldly entities reflected the fact that, at the time, the realms of the cosmos were firmly rooted in superstition and primal fear of the unknown. As scientific knowledge matriculated into society, the overall concept of space changed. No longer was this a quasi-magical realm in which Lovecraftian elder creatures resided. Space instead became a frontier for human exploration. A physical realm that, though strange, was the purvey of human exploration and even colonization. As this occurred, aliens began to become more humanoid in fiction and were thereafter more often used as reflections of humanity and human life than as representations of otherness as might appear in more supernatural fiction.

As humanity's understanding of space has changed, so too has cosmic fiction, becoming more detailed and, in some ways, more conservative in its representations. In the 2010s, there are many "near future" depictions of life in space that utilize familiar, though still fictional, types of technology and depict humanity living in familiar ways, attempting to use space to live more or less recognizable lives, though within fantastic, futuristic settings. Fiction is always a reflection of human ideas, but it also sparks the imagination and inspires individuals to imagine what might be, or how humanity might become. This process reflects scientific endeavor, but also informs it, as the dreams of one generation become the lived reality of the next. Though predictions of the future world nearly always miss the mark in major ways, the process of exchange between imagination and science remains essential fuel for the future realities that will eventually come into being.

Works Used

Anders, Charlie Jane. "Is There Any Plausible Reason Why Aliens Would Evolve to Look Like Us?" *Gizmodo*. Sep 23, 2014. Retrieved from https://io9.gizmodo.com/is-there-any-plausible-reason-why-aliens-would-evolve-t-1638235680.

Branch, Glenn and Craig A. Foster. "Yes, Flat-Earthers Really Do Exist." *Smithsonian*. Oct 24, 2018. Retrieved from https://blogs.scientificamerican.com/observations/yes-flat-earthers-really-do-exist/.

Campion, Nicholas. "How Many People Actually Believe in Astrology?" *The Conversation*. Apr 28, 2017. Retrieved from https://theconversation.com/how-many-people-actually-believe-in-astrology-71192.

McRobbie, Linda Rodriguez. "How Are Horoscopes Still a Thing?" *Smithsonian*. Jan 5, 2016. Retrieved from https://www.smithsonianmag.com/history/how-are-horoscopes-still-thing-180957701/.

"Sci-fi Inventions That Became Reality." *CNN*. Mar 21, 2018. Retrieved from https://www.cnn.com/2018/03/21/health/gallery/sci-fi-inventions-that-became-reality/index.html.

Weisberger, Mindy. "Why Do We Imagine Aliens as 'Little Green Men'?" *Live Science*. Jul 12, 2016. Retrieved from https://www.livescience.com/55370-why-are-aliens-little-green-men.html.

Wolf, Jessica. "The Truth about Galileo and His Conflict with the Catholic Church." *UCLA*. Newsroom. Dec 22, 2016. Retrieved from http://newsroom.ucla.edu/releases/the-truth-about-galileo-and-his-conflict-with-the-catholic-church.

Young, Kevin. "Moon Shot: Race, A Hoax, and the Birth of Fake News." *New Yorker*. Oct 21, 2017. Retrieved from https://www.newyorker.com/books/page-turner/moon-shot-race-a-hoax-and-the-birth-of-fake-news.

Notes

1. Campion, "How Many People Actually Believe in Astrology?"
2. Wolf, "The Truth about Galileo and His Conflict with the Catholic Church."
3. McRobbie, "How Are Horoscopes Still a Thing?"
4. "Sci-fi Inventions That Became Reality," *CNN*.
5. Anders, "Is There Any Plausible Reason Why Aliens Would Evolve to Look Like Us?"
6. Weisberger, "Why Do We Imagine Aliens as 'Little Green Men'?"

Donald Trump's Space Force Plans Analysed by a Sci-Fi Expert

By Paul March-Russell

The Conversation, **August 16, 2018**

The US leadership has plans to introduce a "US Space Force" by 2020. Already announced by president Donald Trump in June, US vice president Mike Pence outlined further details of the plan at a press conference on August 9. The Space Force, he said, would consist of an elite corps of soldiers trained to fight in space, and a space command that would design military strategies for warfare beyond the atmosphere.

Much acrimony and ridicule has ensued, with debates over what such a force could or could not do; the only certainty being that it will cost billions of dollars. Seasoned watchers of both US politics and US science fiction will have had the uncanny feeling, though, of having seen this all before.

The rhetoric of both Pence and Trump, referring respectively to "the boundless expanse of space" and the necessity for "American dominance," is inherently science-fictional, but of a particularly American kind. It is not the cooperatist vision of Soviet science fiction, nor the ramshackled approach of British sci-fi (take *Doctor Who*), and certainly not the Afrofuturist marriage of esoteric technology and indigenous folklore, seen most recently in Ava DuVernay's *A Wrinkle in Time*.

An American Fiction

Instead, it is the projection of the values of Manifest Destiny (that the settler population has an inalienable right to the uncharted lands) into outer space. Not for nothing did Trump's 2020 reelection campaign manager, Brad Parscale, write that Space Force would be "a groundbreaking endeavor for America and the final frontier."

As film and media studies expert, Constance Penley, observed in her 1997 book, *NASA/Trek*, the Cold War politics of the Space Race dovetailed beautifully with the frontier vision of Gene Roddenberry's *Star Trek*. This is particularly true of the pioneer spirit of (to paraphrase the original series' opening words) exploring "strange new worlds," seeking "out new life and new civilisations," and "boldly" going "where no man has gone before."

Roddenberry himself was in a lineage of writers from Edgar Rice Burroughs to Ray Bradbury who, with varying degrees of scepticism, projected frontier values into outer space (most typically, onto the surface of Mars). And as historian

> **To imply that space has only now begun to be militarised glosses over the steady militarization of space since the 1960s... even supporters of the proposal suggest a cyber-hacking force is more necessary.**

Frederic Krome has shown, future war stories published in the US pulps between 1914 and 1945 fed into the cultural and military thinking of how to plan for future conflicts.

Perhaps most bizarrely, the mission to capture Saddam Hussein during the Iraq War was named after John Milius's post-apocalyptic teen movie, *Red Dawn* (1984).

Indeed, the Strategic Defence Initiative (SDI), envisaged by president Ronald Reagan in 1983, not only became known as "Star Wars," but its rhetoric was also derived from science fiction writers such as Ben Bova and Jerry Pournelle. SDI's vision of a circling belt of laser-armed satellites, protecting the US from Soviet attack, chimed perfectly with Pournelle's dream, and with that of other science fiction writers such as Robert Heinlein and Larry Niven—an American renaissance through the militarisation and colonisation of space.

Space Force Rebooted

The current rhetoric of Pence and Trump, in announcing their Space Force, almost exactly echoes the rhetoric of SDI and its then supporters. Both groups posit a pattern of US military decline, under the alleged negligence of previous administrations, in which space, the "natural" home of the US following the moon landings, has been left exposed to foreign aggressors. According to them, it is their enemies, not the US, who have militarised space. And now, they argue, only a show of strength can make space safe again for US democracy.

In this way, the ratcheting-up of an arms race in space is glossed over by a utopian vision, in which the US is regalvanised by dreams of expansion into space—see, for example, the proposed mission to Mars.

There has been genuine concern since 2007, when China shot down one of its own satellites. But to imply that space has only now begun to be militarised glosses over the steady militarisation of space since the 1960s, while even supporters of the proposal suggest a cyber-hacking force is more necessary.

Instead, the proposal for an elite corps of specialised soldiers and strategists sounds more like Heinlein's controversial novel of a fully militarised society, *Starship Troopers* (1959), in which humans are embroiled in a seemingly endless war against the utterly alien "Bugs." There are echoes too of E E Smith's interstellar police force, *Galactic Patrol* (1937), and even the BBC's more low-key *Star Cops* (1987), glumly policing off-world mining colonies in the outer solar system. Of course, the proposal may never take flight—it would still require an Act of Congress—so these more hyperbolic fears and desires may need to be momentarily put aside.

Instead, what we can deduce from the proposal is that we are firmly in the logic of the reboot, that much loved tactic of long-running movie franchises. But, as science fiction scholar Gerry Canavan has argued, the reboot "can show us a story, but can't tell us a plot." Rather than an original and inspiring vision of space exploration, what we have instead here is a meaningless reiteration of past rhetoric that may, quite literally, go nowhere.

Print Citations

CMS: March-Russell, Paul. "Donald Trump's Space Force Plans Analysed by a Sci-Fi Expert." In *The Reference Shelf: New Frontiers in Space,* edited by Micah L. Issitt, 147-149. Amenia, NY: Grey House Publishing, 2019.

MLA: March-Russell, Paul. "Donald Trump's Space Force Plans Analysed by a Sci-Fi Expert." *The Reference Shelf: New Frontiers in Space,* edited by Micah L. Issitt, Grey Housing Publishing, 2019, pp. 147-149.

APA: March-Russell, P. (2019). Donald Trump's space force plans analysed by a sci-fi expert. In Micah L. Issitt (Ed.), *The reference shelf: New frontiers in space* (pp. 147-149). Amenia, NY: Grey Housing Publishing.

The Science of *Star Trek*

David Allen Batchelor
NASA *Goddard Space Flight Center*, July 20, 2016

Original producer Gene Roddenberry and the later writers of the show started with science we know and s-t-r-e-t-c-h-e-d it to fit a framework of amazing inventions that support action-filled and entertaining stories. Roddenberry knew some basic astronomy. He knew that space ships unable to go faster than light would take decades to reach the stars, and that would be too boring for a one-hour show per week. So he put warp drives into the show—propelling ships by distorting the space-time continuum that Einstein conceived. With warp drive the ships could reach far stars in hours or days, and the stories would fit human epic adventures, not stretch out for lifetimes. Roddenberry tried to keep the stars realistically far, yet imagine human beings with the power to reach them. Roddenberry and other writers added magic like the transporter and medical miracles and the holodeck, but they put these in as equipment, as powerful tools built by human engineers in a future of human progress. They uplifted our vision of what might be possible, and that's one reason the shows have been so popular.

The writers of the show are not scientists, so they do sometimes get science details wrong. For instance, there was an episode of *Star Trek: The Next Generation* in which Dr. Crusher and Mr. LaForge were forced to let all of the air escape from the part of the ship they were in, so that a fire would be extinguished. The doctor recommended holding one's breath to maintain consciousness as long as possible in the vacuum, until the air was restored. But as underwater scuba divers know, the lungs would rupture and very likely kill anyone who held his breath during such a large decompression. The lungs can't take that much pressure, so people can only survive in a vacuum if they don't try to hold their breath.

I could name other similar mistakes. I'm a physicist, and many of my colleagues watch *Star Trek*. A few of them imagine some hypothetical, perfectly accurate science fiction TV series, and discredit *Star Trek* because of some list of science errors or impossible events in particular episodes. This is unfair. They will watch Shakespeare without a complaint, and his plays wouldn't pass the same rigorous test. Accurate science is seldom exciting and spectacular enough to base a weekly adventure TV show upon. Generally *Star Trek* is pretty intelligently written and more faithful to science than any other science fiction series ever shown on television. *Star Trek* also attracts and excites generations of viewers about advanced science and engineering, and it's almost the only show that depicts scientists and engineers positively, as role models. So let's forgive the show for an occasional misconception in the service of an epic adventure.

So, what are the features of *Star Trek* that a person interested in science can enjoy without guilt, and what features rightly tick off those persnickety critics? Well, many of the star systems mentioned on the show, such as Wolf 359, really do exist. Usually, though, the writers just make them up. There also have been some beautiful special effects pictures of binary stars and solar flares which were astronomically accurate and instructive. The best accuracy and worst stumbles can be found among the features of the show that have become constant through all of the episodes. Here's a list of the standard *Star Trek* features, roughly in order of increasing scientific incredibility.

Communicators

Like *Star Trek* communicators, cell phones are ubiquitous now, to an annoying extent, and images and videos made with them are now collected and exchanged obsessively. Landing parties in past *Star Trek* shows only gave verbal reports, and did not send back images and videos, as today's people would.

The ship's computer

Today's computers entertain us with video games and movie special effects that are awesomely more spectacular than the special effects in the original *Star Trek* show. Computers also search databases for data about US, mining data to find criminals and terrorists. Mobile computers on rovers explore Mars and deep space for us. Computers today are capable of rendering crude holodeck-like virtual realities, and they enable us to do computer-aided design with great impact on architecture and industry. Supercomputers have advanced the state of the art of modeling weather and climate.

In 400 more years—the time when *Star Trek: The Next Generation* is set—it is reasonable to expect many of the abilities of computers in *Star Trek* to really be achieved. (Interestingly, the Internet was not predicted by *Star Trek* visionaries, who remained focused on large, isolated computers.)

Matter-Antimatter Generation

This is one of the best scientific features of *Star Trek*. The mixing of matter and antimatter is almost certainly the most efficient kind of power source that a starship could use, and the way it's described is reasonably correct—the antimatter (frozen anti-hydrogen) is handled with magnetic fields, and never allowed to touch normal matter, or KA-BOOM! This much is real physics. Let's not bother about the dilithium crystals part . . . sorry, but that's just imaginary.

Antimatter has been created recently in microscopic quantities and is being studied to advance physics knowledge. But it isn't possible yet to produce amounts of antimatter that would be useful for fuel or power generation.

Impulse Engines

These are rocket engines based on the fusion reaction. We don't have the technology for them yet—they are far ahead of our present chemical-fueled rockets—but they are within the bounds of real, possible future engineering.

Some *Star Trek* episodes also mentioned ion drive. In recent decades, Russian, U.S., European, and Japanese spacecraft have used ion drive engines, known as Hall thrusters. They are much more efficient than the usual chemical rockets and have been capable of propelling probes to asteroids and comets in our solar system.

Androids

An important research organization for robotics is the American Association for Artificial Intelligence. At a conference on cybernetics several years ago, the president of the association was asked what is the ultimate goal of his field of technology. He replied, "Lieutenant Commander Data." Creating *Star Trek*'s Mr. Data would be a historic feat of cybernetics, and it's very controversial in computer science whether it can be done. Maybe a self-aware computer can be put into a human-sized body and convinced to live sociably with us and our limitations. That's a long way ahead of our computer technology, but maybe not impossible.

By the way, Mr. Data's "positronic" brain circuits are named for the circuits that Dr. Isaac Asimov imagined for his fictional robots. Our doctors can use positrons to make images of our brains or other organs, but there's no reason to expect that positrons could make especially good artificial brains. Positrons are antimatter! Dr. Asimov just made up a sophisticated-sounding prop, which he never expected people to take literally.

Today there are many kinds of toy robots and remote-controlled machines. However, no artifical minds have been created. The ways that thoughts are encoded and transmitted within the human brain remain only crudely understood, preventing real telepathy from being developed. However, simple brain-to-machine commands can be transmitted, enabling impaired or paralyzed people to control prostheses and machines. Much more complex brain-machine interfaces are in the works.

Alien Beings

The NASA Kepler spacecraft and other astronomical research programs have discovered more than 3,300 planets, as well as nearly 2,500 candidates that need confirmation of the observations. Planets are common in our Galaxy, just as the creators of *Star Trek* believed. There are clear signs that life potentially has numerous home sites in the galaxy. Yet despite much searching, no radio or light transmissions from intelligent civilizations elsewhere in the cosmos have been identified.

Now that we understand biochemistry a little, most scientists now agree that life probably exists in other solar systems. The chemical elements for carbon-based life like the lifeforms on Earth are common in the universe, so maybe lifeforms like ourselves are numerous in the galaxy. We can imagine all kinds of intelligent creatures, with any number of arms, legs, eyes, or antennae—maybe a lot smarter than we are.

It seems doubtful that humanoid shapes would be as common as the alien races on the *Star Trek* shows, but we have to allow the show some concessions to the shapes of available actors. Could half-human/half-alien hybrids

> **Roddenberry and other writers uplifted our vision of what might be possible, and that's the one reason the shows have been so popular.**

ever exist, like Mr. Spock? It seems almost impossible, but with recombinant DNA, our scientists have already created interspecies hybrids. Mr. Spock is not totally beyond biochemical reality, but definitely at the edge.

Sensors and Tricorders

We have vibration sensors, sonar, radar, laser ranging, various kinds of light wavelength detectors and energetic particle detectors, and gravimeters. We also do a little three-dimensional imaging of the interiors of solid objects, like the human body, with magnetic fields and radioactivity detectors. The sensors and tricorders on *Star Trek* are quite different and more revealing as plot devices than anything we have. But with a stretch of the imagination, the tricorder scan could have today's magnetic resonance imager as its ancestor. The Enterprise's sensors must use the more advanced (and imaginary) "subspace fields," when it detects far-away objects in space, because the crew never has to wait for signals to travel to a target at the speed of light and return. Not all of the sensors on the show are possible.

Here on Earth, the LIGO observatory has detected gravitational waves, enabling scientists to study direct observations of faraway colliding stars that had become black holes long ago. The patterns of waves confirm Albert Einstein's gravity theory (the "general" theory of relativity). This is currently the most awesome kind of sensor in modern technology.

Deflector shields, tractor beams, and artificial gravity

We know how to deflect electrically charged objects using electromagnetic fields, and there are concepts for protecting space travelers from cosmic radiation this way. That's the only physics trick we know that resembles the powerful special effects of the *Enterprise*'s shields. We can also make big magnets that have some respectable attraction, and with the right electronic circuits regulating the strength of the magnets, we can imagine towing some kinds of metal objects through space. A beam that is projected at something to attract it is purely imaginary.

Artificial gravity is not about to provide the normal environment of weight that the *Enterprise* crew experience. Specially designed magnetic fields could do a similar, weaker job, but they would play havoc with metal equipment. Try a web search for "levitating frog" to see how it's done, but it's not a feasible, safe substitute for gravity.

We don't have any way to create artificial gravity. Generating artificial graviton particles is imaginable, but there's no way to say how it might be done.

Cloaking devices

Crude cloaking devices have been developed today, but they consist of cumbersome layers of metamaterials that only hide tiny objects from visibility in a limited range of colors. (Metamaterials are made of arrays of tiny electronic devices that combine to produce odd optical properties unlike the usual reflecting and refracting in glass that we are used to.) New varieties of metamaterials undoubtedly will produce new, strange effects, but they don't seem capable of providing complete invisibility.

Subspace communications

Mathematicians discovered the concept of a subspace within a space continuum decades ago, and science fiction writers appropriated the term to serve their needs for a super-advanced way to reach other points in space, time or "other" universes. The concept is alive in physics today, in theories that our space-time may have eleven or more dimensions—three space dimensions and time, plus seven more that are "curled up" within a tiny sub-atomic size scale, where they conveniently explain mysteries of the forces of physics. But *Star Trek* uses its own unrelated version of subspace, with signals that can travel as fast as the fastest starship. This is just a convenient notion to get messages to Star Fleet and back by the end of a TV show, with no realistic physics behind it.

Phaser

According to the *Star Trek: The Next Generation* Technical Manual, phasers are named for PHASed Energy Rectification. They are really just spectacular energy blasters, with no detailed physics explanation. The original concept was that they were the next technological improvement upon LASERs. To the extent that they differ from LASERs, they are just fanciful props, descended from generations of blasters in science fiction of decades past.

Today the army has phaser-like stun weapons, which use microwaves to cause extreme discomfort to skin. LASER weapons are in development and have advanced in capabilities.

Healing rays

Star Trek's Dr. Crusher shines a healing ray on her wounded patients and the skin or bone heals immediately. That's just a magical medical miracle of the imaginary 24th century. Surgeons today do work with lasers to cauterize or seal some tissues, and repair detached retinas. Some dentists use them, too. There is actually a form of adhesive that can stick human cells together like glue and synthetic skin for temporarily protecting wounds. But the body's own healing is usually as fast as any other method. On the other hand, there is some evidence that weak electric currents can accelerate healing of bones, so something similar to Dr. Crusher's procedure - but not instantaneous—may become possible someday.

Replicator

Today, we know how to create microchip circuits and experimental nanometer-scale objects by "drawing" them on a surface with a beam of atoms. We can also suspend single atoms or small numbers of atoms within a trap made of electromagnetic fields, and experiment on them. That's as close as the replicator is to reality. Making solid matter from a pattern, as the replicator appears to do, is pretty far beyond present physics.

Replication of simple structures can be performed today via a technology like multi-layer photo-copying that creates solid objects by building up many layers of hardened fluid. That's not a palatable substitute for an instant cup of "Tea, Earl Grey, hot."

Transporter

We don't have a clue about how to really build a device like the transporter. It uses a beam that is radiated from point A to point B where it STOPS at just the right precise place—even passing through some barriers along the way—and reconstructs the person it carries on the spot. Or it captures a person's pattern, dematerializing him or her, and brings the person to some other point. All of the rematerialized atoms and molecules are somehow in the precisely correct positions, with the right temperatures and adhering together just as if the transportee had not been dematerialized. Rematerializing, why doesn't everything fall to pieces if a gust of wind or just normal gravity disturb the reappearing atoms? Nothing in the physics of today gives a hint about how that might be possible. Arthur C. Clarke's Third Law says, "Any sufficiently advanced technology is indistinguishable from magic." But we can't assume every magical feat could be accomplished, given sufficiently advanced technology.

Today, small numbers of atoms and photons have been teleported. The principal use of this trick will be in quantum computer development, which has the potential to solve extremely complex mathematical problems extremely fast.

The *Star Trek* transporter wasn't used much for one of its greatest powers: space battles, when the transporter would be devastatingly effective at removing patches of the hull of an enemy starship. Maybe that's too easy to fit the show's plots.

Holodeck

Clarke's Third Law applies to this one, too. Holograms are images that appear to have three-dimensional structure. We can't yet imagine a way to assemble matter in the same way as the light in a hologram. We only have some relatively crude virtual reality environments today.

It's interesting that in the original *Star Trek* show, virtual reality was outlawed. Virtual reality invented by advanced aliens (Talosians) destroyed Talosian society by addicting them to endless fantasies. The United Federation of Planets enforced the death penalty on anyone who even *visited* the Talosians. But in *Star Trek: The Next Generation*, virtual reality on the holodeck was treated as a vital form of recreation, and was installed on every large starship to entertain the crew.

Universal language translator

As this is used on the *Star Trek* shows, it's just an automagical device to enable characters to get through the stories. It would be too tedious and repetitious in a one-hour show for the characters to overcome real language barriers in a realistic manner in every show. The way the Enterprise crew can encounter an alien spacecraft, "hail them on standard frequencies," and establish instant telecommunications on their viewscreens is a preposterous shortcut to keep the plot from faltering. We can certainly dismiss the possibility of such an invention ever being built.

Warp Interstellar Drive

This must be the crowning achievement of Federation technology. Despite its fundamental role in the show's plot, it violates known physics to an extent that can't be defended. The detailed explanation of the warp field effect in the *ST: TNG* Technical Manual only raises more questions than it resolves. It is said to involve huge discharges of energy and subspace fields that aren't understood in today's science. However, barring a very unlikely demolition of Einstein's theory by revolutionary discoveries in quantum physics, warp drive can't exist. Physicists of today understand the space-time continuum rather well, and there is very good reason to think that no object can move faster than the speed of light. This doesn't stop scientists like the great expert on relativity and quantum theory, Stephen Hawking, from enjoying the fun of the TV series, however.

Wormhole Interstellar travel and time travel

These are questionable consequences of some mathematical models for extremely bizarre, artificial arrangements of titanic super-massive objects—untested imaginary models where Einstein's relativity theory is stretched to its ultimate limits. We don't have any evidence that Einstein's theory is valid in these theoretical cases, and the arrangements of these giant spinning masses don't occur in nature.

No progress on time travel has occurred to date.

So, the bottom line is: *Star Trek* science is an entertaining combination of real science, imaginary science gathered from lots of earlier stories, and stuff the writers make up week-by-week to give each new episode novelty. The real science is an effort to be faithful to humanity's greatest achievements, and the fanciful science is the playing field for a game that expands the mind as it entertains. The *Star Trek* series are the only science fiction series crafted with such respect for real science and intelligent writing. That's why it's the only science fiction series that many scientists watch regularly . . . like me.

Print Citations

CMS: Batchelor, David A. "The Science of *Star Trek*." In *The Reference Shelf: New Frontiers in Space,* edited by Micah L. Issitt, 150-157. Amenia, NY: Grey House Publishing, 2019.

MLA: Batchelor, David A. "The Science of *Star Trek*." *The Reference Shelf: New Frontiers in Space,* edited by Micah L. Issitt, Grey Housing Publishing, 2019, pp. 150-157.

APA: Batchelor, D. (2019). The science of *Star Trek*. In Micah L. Issitt (Ed.), *The reference shelf: New frontiers in space* (pp. 150-157). Amenia, NY: Grey Housing Publishing.

Would Aliens Look Like Us?

By Jonathan Losos
NPR, October 4, 2007

The universe is teeming with earth-like planets.

In February, three were discovered circling a star, Trappist-1, 40 light years away. Last November, one even closer yet was found—four light years away—orbiting our next-door neighbor, Proxima Centauri. By one estimate, there are as many as 40 billion planets similar to Earth just in our Milky Way galaxy.

With so many potentially habitable exoplanets (as they are called), many believe that it is inevitable that life, even intelligent life, must have arisen on some of them.

But what would those life forms be like?

If we're to believe Hollywood, quite a lot like life here on Earth. From *Star Trek* to *Star Wars* to *Valerian* and beyond, most interplanetary science-fiction movies populate their worlds with lifeforms quite similar—in general appearance and biology—to what has evolved here on Planet Earth. *Guardians of the Galaxy* takes this approach to a new extreme, including Groot, a humanoid evolved from a botanical ancestor (perhaps explaining its limited vocabulary).

Yet, not all films agree. Last year's *Arrival* introduced heptapods, organisms with seemingly little affinity to any species here on the home planet.

So, what should we expect? An *Avatar*-like ecosystem full of species slightly different from those on Earth, or a world composed of unfamiliar organisms?

The great astronomer Carl Sagan was in *Arrival's* camp, proclaiming "extraterrestrials would be very different from us." Paleontologist and evolutionary biologist Stephen Jay Gould expressed similar sentiments, but felt that there was no way to scientifically study the question other than finding life on another planet.

Yet not everyone agrees and, in recent years, the question of how predictable evolution is has become a topic of great scientific inquiry. Convergent evolution is the phenomenon of species independently evolving to be similar. Usually it results from the species adapting to similar situations, natural selection favoring the same solution to the same problem posed by the environment. Convergent evolution was known to Charles Darwin but, until relatively recently, we thought it was uncommon, a great example of the power of natural selection, but not commonplace. We now know, however, that convergence is far from rare; rather, it is pervasive, occurring all around us. Think, for example, of fast-swimming marine predators: dolphins, sharks, tuna and ichthyosaurs (extinct marine reptiles from the Age of the

Dinosaurs) all evolved a very stream-lined body shape and powerful tails for rapid and efficient locomotion. Or consider *Euphorbia* plants from dry parts of Africa. Tough-skinned, often green, with spines instead of leaves, they look like cacti, but they're not—the Old- and New-World doppelgängers have independently evolved the same traits to cope with water loss and herbivores in arid regions.

The pervasiveness of convergence has led some evolutionary biologists to proclaim evolution deterministic, the outcome downright inevitable (see two books by Simon Conway Morris, *Life's Solutions* and *The Runes of Evolution,* and also *Convergent Evolution* by George McGhee). If the environment repeatedly poses the same challenges, and if natural selection repeatedly produces the optimal solutions, then evolution is repeatable. And, as a corollary, we can predict what life would be like on an Earth-like planet—pretty much the same as here. The argument can be taken one step further—the *Homo sapiens* species is supremely adapted to life on Earth, the adaptations we forged as we emerged on the savannahs of Africa proving a brilliant stepping-stone to global dominance. Consequently, if evolution is so deterministic, the expectation for life on planets like our own is clear: Humanoid life forms should evolve and dominate, just like here. Hollywood has it right.

Unfortunately, there's a problem with this argument. Although the list of examples of convergence is impressive, it wouldn't be hard to make an equally impressive list of non-convergence. Off the top of my head, here are some evolutionary singletons, types of animals that have evolved just once, without a close match: sauropod dinosaurs, like *Brontosaurus* (Dinosaur purists may note that the name *Brontosaurus* was long ago discarded, replaced for quirky scientific reasons with

> **If you want to think about what extraterrestrial life might be like, watch *Arrival*, not *Avatar* or *Guardians of the Galaxy*.**

Apatosaurus. To those killjoy know-it-alls I respond, "Haha! Thanks to new scientific discoveries, the name *Brontosaurus* was resurrected in 2015."); elephants; the kiwi; sloths; and the world's greatest animal, the duck-billed platypus. Each of these types of animals has evolved a single time, with no close evolutionary match, now or ever (True: Sauropods and elephants are similar in being huge, lumbering herbivores—but I'm focused on much more similar evolutionary matches).

If evolution is so deterministic, its outcome so predictable, it's hard to understand why there are no matches for these evolutionary singletons. Streams like the ones platypuses inhabit are found on every continent except Antarctica, yet the duckbill hails only from Down Under. Suitable tropical tree branches occur around the world, but sloths only evolved in South America. Why sauropods in the Mesozoic and not today?

The reason is simple: There are actually multiple different ways to solve a problem posed by the environment. Consider the woodpecker and the aye-aye, two completely different animals that live a similar lifestyle, tapping on wood to detect the tunnels of wood-eating grubs, chiseling into the wood to get to the tunnels, then extracting the grubs. But the species have evolved completely different tools to do so, the bird a tough beak, an extremely long tongue covered in prickles, and a skull reinforced against concussions to withstand the repeated jackhammering. The aye-aye, on the other hand, has a long skeletal finger that can twist in any direction and protruding incisors to do the excavating.

We don't need to find life on other planets to test the convergence hypothesis. All we have to do is go to New Zealand, an island on which life has diversified in the absence of terrestrial mammals. If the outcome of natural selection is deterministic, then a world dominated by birds would look pretty much like life elsewhere on the planet. But of course, it doesn't. The kiwi may live a lifestyle similar to a badger, but it doesn't look at all like one. The dominant herbivore is, or was, a 10-foot tall bird (the moa), quite different from deer or bison. Throw in flightless parrots, carnivorous parrots, bats that forage by walking around in the leaf-litter and many more, and we can throw the convergence hypothesis out the window. New Zealand is a distinct evolutionary world, the evolutionary outcome unique.

The question is no longer whether convergence or lack of convergence is common: We know now that both are. Rather, scientists are interested in understanding why convergence occurs in some cases, and not others. It's still early days, but one conclusion is clear: Closely-related species (or populations of the same species) tend to adapt in the same way, not surprisingly because they start out so similar in so many ways—natural selection is likely to modify them in similar ways. By contrast, distantly-related species, initially different in so many attributes, are much more likely to find different ways to adapt to the same situation. Think about the difference between birds and mammals: The former have beaks, the latter teeth and fingers. It's not surprising that woodpeckers and aye-ayes found different ways to solve the same problem.

Of course, life couldn't be more distantly related than if it occurred on another planet. With all the differences that such life forms must exhibit, natural selection (if it occurred—who's to say that evolutionary processes would be the same?) might very well sculpt well-adapted species, but they wouldn't look at all like us and our earthly compatriots. The aye-aye and the kiwi tell us that. And that means that the minority opinion in Hollywood is almost surely correct.

If you want to think about what extraterrestrial life might be like, watch *Arrival*, not *Avatar* or *Guardians of the Galaxy*.

Print Citations

CMS: Losos, Jonathan. "Would Aliens Look Like Us?" In *The Reference Shelf: New Frontiers in Space*, edited by Micah L. Issitt, 158-160. Amenia, NY: Grey House Publishing, 2019.

MLA: Losos, Jonathan. "Would Aliens Look Like Us?" *The Reference Shelf: New Frontiers in Space*, edited by Micah L. Issitt, Grey Housing Publishing, 2019, pp. 158-160.

APA: Losos, J. (2019). Would aliens look like us? In Micah L. Issitt (Ed.), *The reference shelf: New frontiers in space* (pp. 158-160). Amenia, NY: Grey Housing Publishing.

More Than 1 Million People Have RSVP'd to "Storm Area 51" in the Name of Memes

By Allegra Frank
Vox, July 15, 2019

Amid its many failings, Facebook remains good for two things: sending birthday greetings to people you haven't talked to in years, and sharing hilariously inane jokes. Nowhere has that been better exemplified by a public Facebook event that's gone viral due to its bizarre, intentionally meme-friendly premise. More than 1 million people have RSVP'd to ambush Nevada's famed Area 51 this September, an affair whose jokey premise is so deadpan, it has gained some serious mainstream attention.

Early in the week of July 1, the anonymous administrators of the public meme page "Shitposting cause im in shambles" teamed up with a Twitch video game streamer named SmyleeKun to organize an event called "Storm Area 51, They Can't Stop All of Us." Per the event description, attendees are invited to fly out to Lincoln Country, Nevada, and "all meet up at the Area 51 Alien Center tourist attraction and coordinate our entry" at 3 am Pacific on September 20. The goal is supposedly to break into the highly secretive and secure military compound, which has often been characterized in fiction as a place where the US government houses and researches alien technology. The thinking goes that if a bunch of people head toward the high-security base at once, the military won't stand a chance of stopping them.

For added measure, the event description notes, "If we naruto run"—a reference to a highly particular, frequently meme'd style of running from the long-running anime *Naruto*—"we can move faster than their bullets. Lets see them aliens."

The "Storm Area 51" event has gained traction online for its absurdity, drawing reactions across multiple social media platforms. On Twitter, for example, one post that omitted the creators' names—which make it clear that the event is just a high-concept gag—led people who were unfamiliar with its origins to take the idea quite seriously:

The replies to that tweet are full of people making fun of the thousands of Facebook users who have agreed to attend, assuming that they seriously intended to travel out to the famed site in search of extraterrestrial beings. Navigating to the event page, however, reveals that the only thing people are taking seriously is elevating the joke to new heights.

The pinned post to the event's discussion feed, for example, is a poorly drawn, labeled map of the Area 51 site that's meant to be a "game plan." The post calls on participants to join in as either a "Naruto Runner," a "Rock

> **If you aren't fluent in the language of Facebook memes, it's plausible that you could take this event way more seriously than you're intended to.**

Thrower," or a "Kyle" (in reference to yet another, even more convoluted meme), and ends with a plea to any government officials following along.

"Hello US government, this is a joke, and I do not actually intend to go ahead with this plan. I just thought it would be funny and get me some thumbsy uppies on the internet," it reads. "I'm not responsible if people decide to actually storm area 51."

But some serious news outlets have tried to report on the event as if it is something other than a gag assembled by some Very Online 20-somethings for the entertainment of their Very Online peers who love scrolling through memes for hours.

I can't totally blame them. If you aren't fluent in the language of Facebook memes, it's plausible that you could take this event way more seriously than you're intended to. The event description and the page's discussion posts are plastered with shitposting—shorthand for the sharing of especially lowbrow memes. ("Incoherent jokes, hasty Photoshopping, mashups, irrelevance, errors in spelling or grammar—all are hallmarks of the shitpost," as the Daily Dot explained back in 2016.)

This Ridiculous "Event" Is Shitposting at Its Biggest and Best

The beauty of shitposts, commonly found on Facebook, Tumblr, Twitter, Reddit, and pretty much anywhere else millennials have been known to waste time online—lies in how highly shareable they are. Shamelessly silly, these memes are funny mostly for being intentionally lazy, even nonsensical, which makes them good for an eyeroll, snort, and bemused repost to your own page. When you're browsing through a feed as disorganized as Facebook's can be, there's sometimes nothing better than stumbling upon a quick, easy joke.

In part because of most shitposts' intrinsic timelessness—which goes well with Facebook's algorithmic nature—the platform is rife with public and private groups and pages dedicated to shitposts of all types. They're most often inspired by myriad fandoms of innumerable kinds, based on everything from mass transit and video games to essentially any pop culture property you can think of, including *Twin Peaks*, *Pokémon*, and, perhaps most visibly, *The Simpsons*. Jokes about aliens and the like fit right into the shitposting genre; the possible existence of extraterrestrial life is as easy to mock as it is to quibble over.

"Shitposting cause im in shambles" is dedicated to such memes, as its name makes clear. The page's cover photo boasts about hosting "top-tier shitposts," but as a public page that doesn't cater to a specific fandom, it tends to serve as a home for more general interest memes than other, more "focused" shitposting groups. Right now, the page is full of memes based on the Area 51 event, joking about how ludicrous an idea it is. Area 51 also trended on Twitter for several hours, which yielded scores of jokes about what an event involving a bunch of anime fans and alien-seeking Facebook users would look like.

So people on the internet are well aware of the memes, but is the Air Force? The Washington Post set out to find the answer to this question, and was told by a spokesperson that while the Air Force is aware of the proposed Area 51 event, it will not speak to any plans to apprehend participants, should anyone actually show up.

However, its official comments could perhaps fuel attendees' mock paranoia about the Air Force gunning them down during their raid.

"[Area 51] is an open training range for the U.S. Air Force, and we would discourage anyone from trying to come into the area where we train American armed forces," the spokesperson told the Washington Post. "The U.S. Air Force always stands ready to protect America and its assets."

There are two months to go until the Area 51 charge is scheduled to take place, giving the Air Force ample time to suss out the likelihood of this intentionally silly situation. Will the power of shitposting compel somewhere north of a million people to head out to a remote area of the country to peacefully follow through on what is nothing more than a meme? Considering how a defining quality of shitposting is expending an extremely low amount of effort, I'm erring on the side of "no." But I can't deny that I'd love to be wrong.

Print Citations

CMS: Frank, Allegra. "More Than 1 Million People Have RSVP'd to 'Storm Area 51' in the Name of Memes." In *The Reference Shelf: New Frontiers in Space,* edited by Micah L. Issitt, 161-163. Amenia, NY: Grey House Publishing, 2019.

MLA: Frank, Allegra. "More Than 1 Million People Have RSVP'd to 'Storm Area 51' in the Name of Memes." *The Reference Shelf: New Frontiers in Space,* edited by Micah L. Issitt, Grey Housing Publishing, 2019, pp. 161-163.

APA: Frank, A. (2019). More than 1 million people have RSVP'd to "storm area 51" in the name of memes. In Micah L. Issitt (Ed.), *The reference shelf: New frontiers in space* (pp. 161-163). Amenia, NY: Grey Housing Publishing.

Audacious & Outrageous: Space Elevators

By Steve Price

National Aeronautics and Space Administration, September 7, 2000

"Yes, ladies and gentlemen, welcome aboard NASA's *Millennium-Two Space Elevator*. Your first stop will be the Lunar-level platform before we continue on to the New Frontier Space Colony development. The entire ride will take about 5 hours, so sit back and enjoy the trip. As we rise, be sure to watch outside the window as the curvature of the Earth becomes visible and the sky changes from deep blue to black, truly one of the most breathtaking views you will ever see!"

Does this sound like the Sci-Fi Channel or a chapter out of Arthur C. Clarke's, *Fountains of Paradise*? Well, it's not. It is a real possibility—a "space elevator"—that researchers are considering today as a far-out space transportation system for the next century.

David Smitherman of NASA/Marshall's Advanced Projects Office has compiled plans for such an elevator that could turn science fiction into reality. His publication, *Space Elevators: An Advanced Earth-Space Infrastructure for the New Millennium*, is based on findings from a space infrastructure conference held at the Marshall Space Flight Center last year. The workshop included scientists and engineers from government and industry representing various fields such as structures, space tethers, materials, and Earth/space environments.

"This is no longer science fiction," said Smitherman. "We came out of the workshop saying, 'We may very well be able to do this.'"

A space elevator is essentially a long cable extending from our planet's surface into space with its center of mass at geostationary Earth orbit (GEO), 35,786 km in altitude. Electromagnetic vehicles traveling along the cable could serve as a mass transportation system for moving people, payloads, and power between Earth and space.

Current plans call for a base tower approximately 50 km tall—the cable would be tethered to the top. To keep the cable structure from tumbling to Earth, it would be attached to a large counterbalance mass beyond geostationary orbit, perhaps an asteroid moved into place for that purpose.

"The system requires the center of mass be in geostationary orbit," said Smitherman. "The cable is basically in orbit around the Earth."

Four to six "elevator tracks" would extend up the sides of the tower and cable structure going to platforms at different levels. These tracks would allow

---

electromagnetic vehicles to travel at speeds reaching thousands of kilometers-per-hour.

Conceptual designs place the tower construction at an equatorial site. The extreme height of the lower tower section makes it vulnerable to high winds. An equatorial location is ideal for a tower of such enormous height because the area is practically devoid of hurricanes and tornadoes and it aligns properly with geostationary orbits (which are directly overhead).

Equatorial base sites are essential for space elevators because they align properly with geostationary orbits. In Arthur C. Clarke's novel, *Fountains of Paradise*, engineers built a space elevator on the mythical island of Taprobane, which was closely based on Sri Lanka, a real island near the southern tip of India. Clarke made one important change to the geography of Sri Lanka/Taprobane: he moved the island 800 km south so that it straddles the equator. At the moment, Sri Lanka lies between 6 and 10 degrees north.

According to Smitherman, construction is not feasible today but it could be toward the end of the 21st century. "First we'll develop the technology," said Smitherman. "In 50 years or so, we'll be there. Then, if the need is there, we'll be able to do this. That's the gist of the report."

Smitherman's paper credits Arthur C. Clarke with introducing the concept to a broader audience. In his 1978 novel, *Fountains of Paradise*, engineers construct a space elevator on top of a mountain peak in the mythical island of Taprobane (closely based on Sri Lanka, the country where Clarke now resides). The builders use advanced materials such as the carbon nanofibers now in laboratory study.

"His book brought the idea to the general public through the science fiction community," said Smitherman. But Clarke wasn't the first.

As early as 1895, a Russian scientist named Konstantin Tsiolkovsky suggested a fanciful "Celestial Castle" in geosynchronous Earth orbit attached to a tower on the ground, not unlike Paris's Eiffel tower. Another Russian, a Leningrad engineer by the name of Yuri Artsutanov, wrote some of the first modern ideas about space elevators in 1960. Published as a non-technical story in *Pravda*, his story never caught the attention of the West. *Science* magazine ran a short article in 1966 by John Isaacs, an American oceanographer, about a pair of whisker-thin wires extending to a geostationary satellite. The article ran basically unnoticed. The concept finally came to the attention of the space flight engineering community through a technical paper written in 1975 by Jerome Pearson of the Air Force Research Laboratory. This paper was the inspiration for Clarke's novel.

Pearson, who participated in the 1999 workshop, envisions the space elevator as a cost-cutting device for NASA. "One of the fundamental problems we face right now is that it's so unbelievably expensive to get things into orbit," said Pearson. "The space elevator may be the answer."

The workshop's findings determined the energy required to move a payload by space elevator from the ground to geostationary orbit could remain relatively low. Using today's energy costs, researchers figured a 12,000-kg Space Shuttle payload would cost no more than $17,700 for an elevator trip to GEO. A passenger with baggage at 150 kg might cost only $222! "Compare that to today's cost of around $10,000 per pound ($22,000 per kg)," said Smitherman. "Potentially, we're talking about just a few dollars per kg with the elevator."

During the workshop, issues pertinent to transforming the concept from science fiction to reality were discussed in detail. "What the workshop found was there are real materials in laboratories today that may be strong enough to construct this type of system," said Smitherman.

Smitherman listed five primary technology thrusts as critical to the development of the elevator. **First** was the development of high-strength materials for both the cables (tethers) and the tower.

In a 1998 report, *NASA applications of molecular nanotechnology*, researchers noted that "maximum stress [on a space elevator cable] is at geosynchronous altitude so the cable must be thickest there and taper exponentially as it approaches Earth. Any potential material may be characterized by the taper factor—the ratio between the cable's radius at geosynchronous altitude and at the Earth's surface. For steel the taper factor is tens of thousands—clearly impossible. For diamond, the taper factor is 21.9 including a safety factor. Diamond is, however, brittle. Carbon nanotubes have a strength in tension similar to diamond, but bundles of these nanometer-scale radius tubes shouldn't propagate cracks nearly as well as the diamond tetrahedral lattice."

Fiber materials such as graphite, alumina, and quartz have exhibited tensile strengths greater than 20 GPa (Giga-Pascals, a unit of measurement for tensile strength) during laboratory testing for cable tethers. The desired strength for the space elevator is about 62 GPa. Carbon nanotubes have exceeded all other materials and appear to have a theoretical strength far above the desired range for space elevator structures. "The development of carbon nanotubes shows real promise," said Smitherman. "They're lightweight materials that are 100 times stronger than steel."

Once you stop dismissing something as unattainable, then you start working on its development.

The **second** technology thrust was the continuation of tether technology development to gain experience in the deployment and control of such long structures in space.

Third was the introduction of lightweight, composite structural materials to the general construction industry for the development of taller towers and buildings. "Buildings and towers can be constructed many kilometers high today using conventional construction materials and methods," said Smitherman. "There simply has not been a demonstrated need to do this that justifies the expense." Better materials may reduce the costs and make larger structures economical.

Fourth was the development of high-speed, electromagnetic propulsion for mass-transportation systems, launch systems, launch assist systems and high-velocity launch rails. These are, basically, higher speed versions of the trams now used at airports to carry passengers between terminals. They would float above the track, propelled by magnets, using no moving parts. This feature would allow the space elevator to attain high vehicle speeds without the wear and tear that wheeled vehicles would put on the structure.

Fifth was the development of transportation, utility and facility infrastructures to support space construction and industrial development from Earth out to GEO. The high cost of constructing a space elevator can only be justified by high usage, by both passengers and payload, tourists and space dwellers.

During a speech he once gave, someone in the audience asked Arthur C. Clarke when the space elevator would become a reality.

"Clarke answered, 'Probably about 50 years after everybody quits laughing,'" related Pearson. "He's got a point. Once you stop dismissing something as unattainable, then you start working on its development. This is exciting!"

Print Citations

CMS: Price, Steve. "Audacious & Outrageous: Space Elevators." In *The Reference Shelf: New Frontiers in Space,* edited by Micah L. Issitt, 164-167. Amenia, NY: Grey House Publishing, 2019.

MLA: Price, Steve. "Audacious & Outrageous: Space Elevators." *The Reference Shelf: New Frontiers in Space,* edited by Micah L. Issitt, Grey Housing Publishing, 2019, pp. 164-167.

APA: Price, S. (2000). Audacious & outrageous: Space elevators. In Micah L. Issitt (Ed.), *The reference shelf: New frontiers in space* (pp. 164-167). Amenia, NY: Grey Housing Publishing.

Bibliography

Anders, Charlie Jane. "Is There Any Plausible Reason Why Aliens Would Evolve to Look Like Us?" *Gizmodo*. Sep 23, 2014. Retrieved from https://io9.gizmodo.com/is-there-any-plausible-reason-why-aliens-would-evolve-t-1638235680.

Bacevich, Andrew J. "Op-Ed: Trump's Ridiculous Space Force Is—Sadly—an Extension of America's Existing National Security Strategy." *Los Angeles Times*. Jun 21, 2018.

Bachman, Justin and Travis Tritten. "Why Trump Wants a Space Force for the Final Frontier." *The Washington Post*. Feb 19, 2019. Retrieved from https://www.washingtonpost.com/business/why-trump-wants-a-space-force-for-the-final-frontier/2019/02/19/aac0b1ee-349d-11e9-8375-e3dcf6b68558_story.html?noredirect=on.

Branch, Glenn, and Craig A. Foster. "Yes, Flat-Earthers Really Do Exist." *Smithsonian*. Oct 24, 2018. Retrieved from https://blogs.scientificamerican.com/observations/yes-flat-earthers-really-do-exist/.

Brinkmann, Paul. "U.S. Should Skip Moon, Head for Mars, Apollo 11's Michael Collins Says." *UPI*. Jul 15, 2019. Retrieved from https://www.upi.com/Top_News/US/2019/07/15/US-should-skip-moon-head-for-Mars-Apollo-11s-Michael-Collins-says/5701563151864/.

Campion, Nicholas. "How Many People Actually Believe in Astrology?" *The Conversation*. Apr 28, 2017. Retrieved from https://theconversation.com/how-many-people-actually-believe-in-astrology-71192.

Chan, Minnie. "Why Donald Trump's New Space Force Can't Hurt China Like Star Wars Hurt the Soviet Union." *South China Morning Post*. Oct 4, 2018. Retrieved from https://www.scmp.com/news/china/military/article/2166844/why-donald-trumps-new-space-force-cant-hurt-china-star-wars-hurt.

Dvorsky, George. "Humans Will Never Colonize Mars." *Gizmodo*. Jul 30, 2019. Retrieved from https://gizmodo.com/humans-will-never-colonize-mars-1836316222.

Erwin, Sandra. "Defense Intelligence Report: China in Steady Pursuit of Space Capabilities to Outmatch U.S." *Space News*. Jan 16, 2019. Retrieved from https://spacenews.com/defense-intelligence-report-china-on-steady-pursuit-of-space-capabilities-to-outmatch-u-s/.

"Europa Lander." *JPL*. NASA Jet Propulsion Laboratory. 2019. Retrieved from https://www.jpl.nasa.gov/missions/europa-lander/.

Fernholz, Tim. "Virgin Galactic Makes It to Space." *Quartz*. Dec 13, 2018. Retrieved from https://qz.com/1494884/richard-bransons-virgin-galactic-reaches-space/.

"The Future." *NASA*. 2019. Retrieved from https://www.nasa.gov/specials/60counting/future.html.

George, Alice. "The Sad, Sad Story of Laika, the Space Dog, and Her One-Way Trip into Orbit." *Smithsonian*. Apr 11, 2018.

Glass, Andrew. "President Reagan Calls for Launching 'Star Wars' Initiative, March 23, 1983." *Politico*. Mar 23, 2017. Retrieved from https://www.politico.com/story/2017/03/president-reagan-calls-for-launching-star-wars-initiative-march-23-1983-236259.

Howell, Elizabeth. "Orion Spacecraft: Taking Astronauts Beyond Earth Orbit." *Space*. Nov 20, 2018. Retrieved from https://www.space.com/27824-orion-spacecraft.html.

Howell, Joe T., and John C. Mankins. "Preliminary Results from NASA's Space Solar Power Exploratory Research and Technology Program." *NTRS*. Jan 01, 2000. Retrieved from https://ntrs.nasa.gov/search.jsp?R=20000044328.

Insinna, Valerie. "Trump Officially Organizes the Space Force under the Air Force... for Now." *Defense News*. Feb 19, 2019. Retrieved from https://www.defensenews.com/space/2019/02/19/trump-signs-off-on-organizing-the-space-force-under-the-air-forcefor-now/.

"John F. Kennedy Moon Speech—Rice Stadium." *NASA*. Retrieved from https://er.jsc.nasa.gov/seh/ricetalk.htm.

Kernan, Michael. "The Space Race." *Smithsonian*. Aug 1997. Retrieved from https://www.smithsonianmag.com/history/the-space-race-141404095/.

Kluger, Jeffrey. "What Sarah Brightman's 'Postponed' Mission Says About Space Tourism." *Time*. May 13, 2015. Retrieved from https://time.com/3857685/sarah-brightman-space-tourism-mission/.

Kluger, Jeffrey. "Why Trump's 'Space Force' Won't – and Shouldn't – Happen." *Time*. Jun 19, 2018. Retrieved from https://time.com/5316007/space-force-trump/.

Larimer, Sarah. "'We Have a Fire in the Cockpit!' The Apollo 1 Disaster 50 Years Later." *The Washington Post*. Jan 26, 2017. Retrieved from https://www.washingtonpost.com/news/speaking-of-science/wp/2017/01/26/50-years-ago-three-astronauts-died-in-the-apollo-1-fire/.

Lovell, Jim. "Houston, We've Had a Problem," *Apollo Expeditions to the Moon*. NASA. Retrieved from https://history.nasa.gov/SP-350/ch-13-1.html.

Mann, Adam. "Space Tourism to Accelerate Climate Change." *Nature*. Oct 22, 2010. Retrieved from https://www.nature.com/news/2010/101022/full/news.2010.558.html.

"MARS 2020 Mission." *NASA*. 2019. Retrieved from https://mars.nasa.gov/mars2020/.

McRobbie, Linda Rodriguez. "How Are Horoscopes Still a Thing?" *Smithsonian*. Jan 5, 2016. Retrieved from https://www.smithsonianmag.com/history/how-are-horoscopes-still-thing-180957701/.

Nankivell, Kirk. "Why the Future of Solar Power Is from Space." *Singularity Hub*. Dec 31, 2018. Retrieved from https://singularityhub.com/2018/12/31/why-the-future-of-solar-power-is-from-space/.

"NASA's Plans to Explore Europa and Other 'Ocean Worlds'." *Phys Org.* Mar 6, 2017. Retrieved from https://phys.org/news/2017-03-nasa-explore-europa-ocean-worlds.html.

Pappalardo, Joe. "A 10-Year Odyssey: What Space Stations Will Look Like in 2030." *Popular Mechanics.* Jun 10, 2019. Retrieved from https://www.popularmechanics.com/space/satellites/a27886809/future-of-iss-space-station/.

Porter, Jon. "Virgin Galactic to Become the First Space Tourism Company to Go Public." *The Verge.* Jul 9, 2019. Retrieved from https://www.theverge.com/2019/7/9/20687323/virgin-galactic-publicly-traded-richard-branson-space-tourism-profitability.

Portree, David S. "Dreaming a Different Apollo." *Wired.* Oct 13, 2014. Retrieved from https://www.wired.com/2014/10/dreamingadifferentapollo/.

Powell, Corey S. "The ISS Was Never Supposed to End Like This." *MACH.* NBC News. Feb 22, 2018. Retrieved from https://www.nbcnews.com/mach/science/iss-was-never-supposed-end-ncna848771.

Redd, Nola Taylor. "Alan Shepard: First American in Space." *Space.* Oct 10, 2018.

Rinehart, Will. "The Options for the Future of the International Space Station." *American Action Forum.* Sep 25, 2018.

Sagdeev, Roald, and Susan Eisenhower. "United States-Soviet Space Cooperation during the Cold War." *NASA.* Retrieved from https://www.nasa.gov/50th/50th_magazine/coldWarCoOp.html.

Schlosser, Eric. "The Growing Dangers of the New Nuclear-Arms Race." *New Yorker.* May 24, 2018. Retrieved from https://www.newyorker.com/news/news-desk/the-growing-dangers-of-the-new-nuclear-arms-race.

"Sci-fi Inventions That Became Reality." *CNN.* Mar 21, 2018. Retrieved from https://www.cnn.com/2018/03/21/health/gallery/sci-fi-inventions-that-became-reality/index.html.

Shieber, Jonathan. "Space Force Will Be a Marines-Like Branch under Air Force Authority." *Tech Crunch.* Retrieved from https://techcrunch.com/2019/02/19/marines-in-space/.

Sowers, George. "Commercializing Space: Before a Commercial LEO Market Can Flourish, the ISS Must Be Retired." *Space News.* Mar 19, 2019. Retrieved from https://spacenews.com/op-ed-commercializing-space-before-a-commercial-leo-market-can-flourish-the-iss-must-be-retired/.

Tamblyn, Thomas. "NASA Unveils Its First Spaceplane Since the Shuttle." *Huffington Post.* Aug 25, 2017. Retrieved from https://www.huffingtonpost.co.uk/entry/nasa-unveils-its-first-spaceplane-since-the-shuttle_uk_59a01123e4b0821444c29987?guccounter=1.

"The Truman Doctrine, 1947." *U.S. Department of State.* Office of the Historian. 2016. Retrieved from https://history.state.gov/milestones/1945-1952/truman-doctrine.

"U.S. Defense Spending Compared to Other Countries." *PGPF.* Peter G. Peterson Foundation. May 3, 2019. Retrieved from https://www.pgpf.org/chart-archive/0053_defense-comparison.

Weisberger, Mindy. "Why Do We Imagine Aliens as 'Little Green Men'?" *Live Science*. Jul 12, 2016. Retrieved from https://www.livescience.com/55370-why-are-aliens-little-green-men.html.

Whitcomb, Isobel. "NASA Wants to Let Space Tourists Onto the Space Station—for $59 Million." *Live Science*. Jun 7, 2019. Retrieved from https://www.livescience.com/65670-nasa-iss-space-tourism.html.

Wolf, Jessica. "The Truth About Galileo and His Conflict with the Catholic Church." *UCLA*. Newsroom. Dec 22, 2016. Retrieved from http://newsroom.ucla.edu/releases/the-truth-about-galileo-and-his-conflict-with-the-catholic-church.

Young, Kevin. "Moon Shot: Race, a Hoax, and the Birth of Fake News." *New Yorker*. Oct 21, 2017. Retrieved from https://www.newyorker.com/books/page-turner/moon-shot-race-a-hoax-and-the-birth-of-fake-news.

Websites

Air Force Space Command

www.afspc.af.mil

The Air Force Space Command is the branch of the U.S. Air Force charged with managing the defense of American assets in space. As of 2019, the Trump Administration's "Space Force" will be managed and overseen by the Air Force Space Command division, which was established in 1982 and has since been managing space defense programs for the United States, essentially filling the same role as the proposed "Space Force" was intended to subsume.

American Astronomical Society (ASS)

www.aas.org

The American Astronomical Society is a professional society representing astronomers and others in the field of space science. The organization actively promotes the establishment and development of space science programs for professionals and astronomy education at various levels of the American education system. The AAS is the oldest astronomical society in the nation, having been first established in 1899 by pioneering American astronomer George Ellery Hale.

National Aeronautics and Space Administration (NASA)

www.nasa.gov

The National Aeronautics and Space Administration is an independent, civilian agency within the United States established in 1958 for the purposes of overseeing and managing American space science and exploration. NASA is one of the earliest and largest space exploration organizations in the world and works closely with academic and other organizations to fund and participate in research on extraterrestrial life, the physics and chemistry of space, and issues involving space exploration.

NASA Jet Propulsion Laboratory (JPL)

www.jpl.nasa.gov

NASA's Jet Propulsion Laboratory is a research center located in California and established in the 1930s to manage development of propulsion systems for rockets and aircraft. In the twenty-first century, programs at NASA's JPL, which is managed in conjunction with the California Institute of Technology, works on a wide variety of programs involving space technology, including robotics and automation and deep space research and monitoring programs. NASA's JPL teams are responsible for a variety of NASA's best-known programs, including the construction of earth and orbital telescope equipment and the famous rover programs that enabled scientists to explore the surface of Mars.

Office for Outer Space Affiars (UNOOSA)
www.unoosa.org

The United Nations Office for Outer Space Affairs (UNOOSA) is a branch of the UN Secretariat responsible for enforcing the international agreements that were part of the United Nations Committee on the Peaceful Uses of Outer Space. Started in 1958, UNOOSA hosts intergovernmental discussions on scientific, military, and private projects and programs that impact outer space and also assists other nations in developing space technology.

The Planetary Society
www.planetary.org

The Planetary Society, founded in 1980 by internationally renowned astronomer Carl Sagan and colleagues, is an international nonprofit organization that advocates for space and planetary science research and supports public education and advocacy programs. The Planetary Society is one of the world's first private space-science nongovernmental organizations, and is focused on supporting the exploration of the solar system and the search for extraterrestrial life. In addition to Sagan, well-known members of the organization include Louis Friedman, science-educator Bill Nye, and Neil DeGrasse Tyson.

Space Foundation
www.spacefoundation.org

The Space Foundation is a U.S.-based nonprofit that advocates for the national space industry by creating and presenting educational events. The Space Foundation offers pre–K-20 programs that include science, technology, engineering, and mathematics (STEM), astronomy, and other space-science-based learning programs. Annually, the Space Foundation hosts a Space Symposium in Colorado that invites specialists in various space science related fields from around the world and showcases new technology from both private and public manufacturing firms.

SpaceX
www.spacex.com

SpaceX, or Space Exploration Tehcnologies Corp. is a private, California-based aerospace manufacturing and space tourism company founded in 2002 by controversial billionaire Elon Musk. SpaceX launched the first privately constructed liquid-propellant rocked into space and was the first private company to send a spacecraft into orbit and to visit the International Space Station (ISS). The company helped initiate public interest in space tourism, but has also been engaged in controversial activities, such as the 2018 launch of a Tesla Roadster vehicle to orbit the sun, the first object dispatched from earth for this unusual purpose. SpaceX has been engaged in a partnership with NASA, aiding the organization in bringing supplies to the International Space Station.

Virgin Galactic

www.virgin galactic.com

Virgin Galactic is a leading company in the burgeoning "space tourism" industry. Started by British business investor Richard Branson, Virgin Galactic suffered a major setback in 2014 with the loss of the company's *VSS Enterprise* ship, and the death of one of the vehicle's two pilots, but has since made significant strides to regain a position as a leader in the field, becoming the second company to achieve space flight with a privately designed ship and the first space tourism company to go public in 2019.

Index